Don't Forget Your Crown

Self-love has everything to do with it

Derrick Jaxn

Printed in the United States of America

First Printing, 2018

ISBN: 978-0-9910336-7-6

Shop Derrick Jaxn LLC

derrickjaxn.com

Contents

Introduction

Some of you know me as the Self-Love Ambassador, a moniker I felt better suited me than the "love guru" label that latches onto you the moment you voice your perspective on relationships.

While by its technical definition of someone who guides and mentors others in a particular area of life, I would, in fact, be considered a guru, the implication behind that term is that one knows everything, and I'd be the first to tell you I do not. I just know a few things are undeniable, and our society hasn't learned, yet, to stop trying to deny them.

For example, there's no need for a guy to lie and deceive if all he wants is sex. Many women want the same thing, and it could save everyone a lot of trouble if intentions were made clear from the beginning. Or the fact that, yes, women are "emotional creatures," but so are men. We just show it differently or let it build up and all come out at once to the bewilderment of the woman whom we'd been telling we were just fine the entire time.

Probably the most undeniable of all is that without self-love, no love matters. It can be poured into us endlessly, but with our broken cup, we'll still be left empty in the end. The list goes on, but you get the point.

However, I did not. Not until it was too late.

On the first day of the spring semester in my sophomore year in college, at age nineteen, I met my future wife, Da'Naia. It took me a week to realize it, although I spent several months trying to fight the realization. But I couldn't. She understood me better than my own mother. She could relate to me better than any best friend I'd ever had. She intrigued me more than any passion I'd discovered. She was fair and kind in how she dealt with others, but she didn't take shit. She was conservative in how she carried herself, but open-minded enough to have fun. She was just imperfect enough to be called a human, but more than perfect enough for me.

Sound beautiful? Well, it was. About as beautiful as a brand-new Lamborghini. The problem came when the keys to it were handed to someone who mentally didn't even have his learner's permit, me. I ran red lights, went the wrong way down one-ways, sped up over potholes, and eventually, you guessed it, wrecked.

It wasn't my original plan, but for lack of planning for anything else, it was inevitable despite trying to learn on the job how to handle the luxury vehicle that'd been put in my possession.

I consulted with friends who turned out not to know any better than I did, and even read dozens of relationship self-help books, but not only were they a complete snooze, most of them were either really preachy or outdated and impractical.

Preachy advice made everything strictly about what was morally right and wrong, not really a how-to for someone who'd never had any experience. It's nice to know that a destination is beautiful, but it doesn't help if there's no map or GPS detailing how to get there.

Outdated and impractical advice spoke as if we were in the 1920s, before there was social media, an oversexualized society, and women who no longer wanted to stay home and scrub wood panel floors on their knees while the man went to work at the steel mill.

Although relationships lasted longer back then, today's world is much different, and standards for men are rightfully higher. We can't just bring home the bacon and our job is done. Women today are bringing home their own bacon and want a man who'll inquire about their day without having to beg him to. They also like flowers every now and then, the ability to have a say-so about decisions that'll affect the family they're responsible for increasing, and a man who's willing to be emotionally vulnerable instead of just sexually available.

But it was through those books, friend-to-friend consultations, and quests to find out exactly how this whole relationship thing worked that I heard things like, "A man gon' be a man." "Sometimes a woman's purpose in a man's life is to prepare him for the next woman." "All men cheat, even the good ones." "If she loves you enough, she'll forgive anything."

And it was through experience with a sprinkle of common sense that I learned almost all of it was garbage. The rest just needed to join us in the twenty-first century, and I volunteered myself as chauffeur by way of viral online videos and posts a few years ago.

Did I become an expert? By my measure, not really, although tens of millions of people who continue to gain value from my videos every week would suggest otherwise. I just don't think we need any more of the hand-me-down ideologies that got dating and relationships into the trouble they're in now.

What we need is a brutally honest fact-check on all the normalized bullshit we've been following and in which we've been failing for decades yet expecting different results the longer we continue. That includes the media's false advertising, social media's relationship goals, pastors' sermons, grannies' wisdom, and yes, even some of our favorite experts' expertise.

What we need is a complete overhaul and fundamental insertion of self-love, and that's where I come in. After it fixed my wrecked Lamborghini, it's the least I could do to return the favor.

CHAPTER 1

❖

A Man Will Act Right for the Right Woman

If hormones were animals, mine were a pack of wild dogs--a step above lions in terms of domesticity, but far from being sophisticated enough to be anyone's house pet. I never once considered grooming them since they were perfect for the newly legal bachelor life I was living when I began college, and while I never thought about how it would affect a serious relationship, in the back of my mind I figured the right woman would inspire the qualities I needed to function in one. But for the time being, my job was to be as sexually uninhibited as possible, get to class on time, and stay out of jail.

My sophomore year, there was a wrench thrown in my plans when I saw a gorgeous brown-skinned girl with full lips and curvy hips walk through the door into my math class. The wrench was because she didn't too much exude sex, and the feeling that I got wasn't the familiar one of lust, but there was somewhat of an aura I was yet intrigued by.

I approached the young lady after class and asked for her number. She told me her name was Da'Naia, then hesitantly took my phone and entered her contact info. Maybe it was just to be nice or because she had things to do and didn't feel like small talking, but to me, it didn't matter.

Two un-replied-to text messages and a third and final attempt to call her later, we had our first real conversation, and it was on from there.

We clicked, instantly and consistently, over the following months. Her aura had not misled me one bit in convincing me she was a dope individual, and I made up my mind that I didn't want her to be anyone else's, which inadvertently meant, it was time for me to be all hers, as well.

That's when it happened. "The switch" flipped, with me transforming into a relationship-ready man like all the guys do in love stories. My eyes that once wandered across the sea of women around me were now only for her. My temper became non-existent for anything she did that rubbed me the wrong way. No matter if she had a bad hair day, dressed down, or had bags under her eyes from not getting much sleep, I saw a perfect ten out of ten when I looked at her. "This is it," I thought to myself. I'd met the right woman, and all the changes she was responsible for making within me had finally happened.

Well, I couldn't have been higher if I'd drunk crack cocaine through a sippy cup. I was not ready for a relationship, and nothing changed inside me. I was experiencing the honeymoon phase that would expire a short while later when we had our first argument, and neither of us felt like we were wrong. Of course, being the emotionally immature person I was, that meant silent treatment, and the euphoric dust settled, revealing the same "me" that I came into the relationship as.

We eventually got over that hump, but the next two years were tumultuous, with me being at the eye of the hurricane in most of our drama. I was still in love, no doubt about it, but as for the love I was to invest into the relationship, I was ill-prepared for the job. If she did anything that upset me, regardless if she was right or wrong, I withdrew. When she didn't see things my way, I pridefully ignored her perspective. I wanted to hang out as much as I did when I was single but expected her availability when it was convenient for me. I would do occasionally thoughtful things, but not consistently. Even the compliments I gave her would be beyond expired by the time I came around to giving her another, yet I felt jealousy when I saw other guys giving her the attention she wanted from me, despite her ignoring it. To make matters worse, I swore to myself I would never cheat, but I was as much of an infidel as anyone else with the way I flirtatiously carried on with other girls, blaming it on my personality instead of my inconsideration.

She made her mistakes from time to time, but without them, we'd still have been in a downward spiral by my actions, which, by the way, were on a completely different page than my intentions. Ironically, I held the belief that if a person really wanted to act consistently in a certain manner, it would just happen. Never mind behavioral psychology, deeply rooted habits, maturity, and years of conditioning. Sincere intentions would override all of that, immediately, so I thought.

But the reality was, I was living out the proof that the saying, "A man will act right for the right woman" was false. This had nothing to do with her being right, but everything to do with me being wrong, and subconsciously I didn't bring myself to accept that truth until it was too late.

My actions were a direct reflection of the work I did to get ready for her, or lack thereof, just like anyone else in any other situation. Harvard University professor of psychology B.F. Skinner explains this as structuralism in his book, *About Behaviorism*, but we don't have to get so technical with practical examples all around us.

Take Beyonce, for example. She doesn't shut down Coechella with an all-time great performance because it's the right stage. She hits every dance move on beat, sings every note in tune, and looks good doing it because of the years of fine-tuning her skills and rehearsals leading up to the performance. Maybe she misses some steps behind the scenes or was out of shape beforehand, but when the time comes she executes and it has nothing to do with the microphone, size of the event, weather, or TV stations that would be broadcasting. She knew long before what her goals were and committed to the work necessary to show up when the opportunity came.

Long-distance track Olympians don't "run right" for the right competition. They train for years by lifting, managing their body weight, working on their running mechanics, and when the time comes, all their hard work is simply put on display. Even with the best intentions, purest love for their sport, and their entire future on the line, the single deciding factor in those athletes being able to finish a twenty-six-mile run, and compete at the highest level while doing it, was their preparation.

While God-given talent can play a part, that's not due much credit either. For instance, Usain Bolt, who's undoubtedly one of the most naturally gifted athletes of all time, would not have won a single gold medal if he sat on his couch and played NBA 2K every day while throwing back shots of liquor and eating Waffle House. Yes, he had the size and genetics that few are blessed with, but it was what he did with those qualities beforehand that made the difference in him becoming the fastest man to ever walk the Earth.

Some men are "naturally gifted" with creativity, compassion, work ethic, romantic inclination, and other qualities that would make a woman feel like the luckiest person alive, but due to the decision not to work on themselves before meeting her, those men make their woman regret the day she chose not to ignore him.

Does this apply to women in relationships? Sure it does, but most times, that's not quite how the story goes. In most cultures, a woman is "trained" for a relationship from a young age. She's taught how to cook and clean by a mom who sees it her duty to instill those domestic qualities in her, or else a man won't want her. She's taught to be conservative with her sexuality because Dad refuses to raise a "harlot." She's inundated with how much better or validated her life will be when she gets married with every romance novel, movie, and song she listens to, then grows up to realize it takes two to tango, and the other half of this equation has been getting trained for a completely different sport, the sport of being "players."

So, while these women aren't perfect, their relationship preparation would generally give them an advantage over men who weren't equipped with the same tools to win, but with no referees, it only leaves them subject to injury. Imagine Lebron James playing a full-speed pickup game with a team of aspiring wrestlers. Even if those wrestlers mean well, Lebron's more than likely walking into a dangerous situation.

The same happens when women do wifey things for boys who've only been prepped to look for a good time, not a lifetime. Instead of needing to prepare better for her relationship like men, she now has to figure out how to repair from the relationship with boys she mistook as men. This is the part left out of the young-girl-growing-up training manual, and this is where many women miss their blessings because they either adjust their standards for men down to match them in their brokenness or miss out on men they really deserve because he realizes she hasn't healed from her past enough to fulfill him in a healthy relationship.

Therefore, "A man will act right for the right woman" is not only false, but an unhealthy narrative to continue propagating. With this mindset, men will continue being unprepared for relationships, and women will continue hurting themselves in efforts to love unprepared men or even worse, spending their best years preparing him for the next woman.

This has become the case so often. Some believe it can be a woman's purpose to prepare a man for another woman. However, outside of his mother, no, a woman's purpose is never to give the best of her love, get her hopes up, invest her energy and precious time into a man, just to be left to see him take that and give to another woman while she's left to pick up the pieces to her heart. This is the small print we don't read between the lines of, "Prepare him."

While those may be the ways she benefits him, that's never the purpose of any woman, and believing so is to tell the woman who is used for her upgrading capabilities yet left with nothing but a broken heart that it was supposed to be that way. Imagine telling a scuba diver who nearly drowns from a defective air tank that the tank's purpose was to make him a better swimmer. Imagine telling slaves their purpose was to jump start America with free labor for a great economy. Both of those are equally as ridiculous as telling a woman her and her heart's purpose was being a man's practice facility.

This is another reason we must retire these bogus notions that give birth to others, and possibly more erroneous ones. They tend to be at the core of the belief that when it comes to our shortcomings as men, someone else is either to blame, or we shouldn't be held but so accountable for them because that's the way the world is supposed to work.

We're allowed to remain convinced that our behavior in dealings with women is a matter of being uninspired to do better by the quality of who she is instead of a measure of who we are, regardless of who she is. What does that result in? Years later, still blaming every woman we meet for never growing up or remembering that we let a "good one" get away due to our flawed logic nobody taught us better than.

I was on the path to being one of those men, but I couldn't ignore the obvious. For any excuse I was tempted to hide behind as to what led to my fuckboy behavior, the root always led back to me.

Yes, I was raised in a single-parent household. Yes, most guys my age and even much older were doing the same things. Yes, we're all "imperfect." But, no, those things don't excuse the fact I accepted my girl's heart under conditions that I didn't honor. They don't excuse the fact that when I became unhappy, I handled it by being disloyal instead of leaving. They don't change the fact that if for whatever reason, she did the same things to me that I did to her, I wouldn't care to hear what reasons she did them for. I would be gone, for good. So, it was time to make a change.

CHAPTER 2

Unconditional Love is Dangerous

They say hindsight is 20/20, but I believe the concept only applies when you're looking back through a lens of honesty, not through a conversation with your boy who's no better than you and may even be a little worse.

"She said no matter what, she would always love you, though." "All relationships go through things." "She just up and left as soon as things got hard?" This was the feedback I got from a chat with my friend Calvin after my breakup with Da'Naia. He was the last person I should've called to try and fix my life at the time it all went down, but he was available, so there we were.

Although he didn't help me get to the answers I was originally looking for, I did make a discovery that day. As he kept talking about how he couldn't believe that a girl could ever leave from being mistreated, I began to see more and more why the unconditional love thing was another flawed belief. Honestly, the mere fact that he believed in it should've been enough of a red flag, but other than the love a mother or father has for their child, or for a person loving themselves, unconditional love has done more harm than good, and would benefit anyone who abandoned the idea of it.

For clarity, I'm not referring to love as the fuzzy feeling most people characterize it as, but love as an action verb. The application, display, and consistent investment into your partner to grow with and manifest the best in them; that love should only be given with conditions, and this is why.

In my teenage years and even into my early twenties, loving my girlfriend felt like trying to fly a plane while intoxicated. Sober, I would've failed miserably because I had no idea how to fly a plane, but being drunk only made the crash come quicker. I didn't know how to love, really had never witnessed it in action, but the fact that I had major pride issues and a botched definition of loyalty only made things worse. Whereas staying out all night without letting her know where I was going and how long I was going to be out would be a problem fixable by a little compromise, my pride told me that as a man, I had no obligation to check in with my girl. I was free to do as I pleased so long as I didn't cheat.

My pride also told me that so long as I worked and paid the bills, my work was done. If she got tired, that was her slacking and not something I needed to concern myself with. The support and emotional presence she needed from me was not on my priority list. Therefore, I never gave her the helping hand a teammate is supposed to.

My definition of loyalty was undoubtedly the biggest issue. Initially, I viewed it as something she needed to display in the form of sexual purity; the utmost reverence for my insecurities when engaging with any other man for any reason; and granting me all access to her phone, social media, email, or whatever else would normally have a password just in case I got curious. I also wanted to be made aware of all advances from other men, so I could keep them on my radar. This was the easy way out of having to trust her that she'd given me no reason not to.

But as for my definition of loyalty that I had to abide by, yes, there was a separate meaning for me; it meant *trying* not to screw other girls and doing a good enough job at hiding it should I ever "slip up". Being that this was my first attempt at even considering sexual discipline, I granted myself privileges I had no business granting myself.

Yes, consciously, I knew better, but post-honeymoon phase, this seemed like the most feasible option to maintain my relationship and keep me out of trouble until I mastered the real thing--a foolish thought to say the least.

While I didn't have sex with any other girl until the end of the relationship, there was enough talk about how I was being flirtatious with several around campus and sketchy behavior she witnessed firsthand to put two and two together that I wasn't being respectful of the relationship.

For instance, my phone being tucked away when I wanted to text and ringing late at night while I just silenced it and acted like it was nothing. Her not hearing from me for two or three days when we had an argument; those things would set off her Spidey senses. She'd go through my phone, see how I was carrying on with different girls, and I'd promise to do better when she brought it to my attention.

For about a month of the emotional low of feeling like a complete scum-bag, I would, and then I'd regress back to a modified version of the disloyalty I exhibited before. This time around, instead of five or six girls, now just one or two, and I kept them at a cordial distance while my relationship was on good terms instead of officially burning the bridge as I was supposed to.

Without checking my ego, it remained so fragile that I relied on a safety net of other girls I could access to coddle me in times I wanted to feel right even if I was wrong. So, any argument Da'Naia and I had sent me fleeing into the emotional comfort of other girls who'd only hear my side of the story and remind me of how right I was instead of handling my domestic issues internally with the one who had everything invested in the relationship. That emotional comfort turned into flirting, which would grow into side-situationships, just without the sex.

At the time, my friend Calvin thought if this wasn't loyalty, it was close enough, and I bought into the same stupidity so I could sleep at night. Except loyalty isn't one of those things you simply get close to doing right. It's something you either are or you are not, and I was no different from anyone else who cheated. I had her looking foolish for trusting me. I showed no regard for my relationship, and the peace of mind she was never afforded because of how I conducted myself became a living hell for her at times. The worst part of it all is that the entire time, I was still receiving her love, unconditionally, and she eventually paid a high price to give it to me.

She continued being there for me, holding in the hurt that she was feeling, hoping it would just go away. She continued trying to satisfy me physically and understand me emotionally despite me being distant. She continued rejecting the guys who wanted her, and she stayed in even on weekends when I was out at different parties. She continued loving me, and it took such a toll on her that over time, she was no longer the girl I originally met.

With every argument after which she knew I was running off to talk with other girls, she became less of herself. Moods were unpredictable, then worsened to being unmanageable. She was perpetually unhappy because she was in pain. She didn't voice her concerns because she didn't have enough concrete evidence of what she knew deep down that I was doing, but that didn't stop it from impacting her.

I noticed something was up, but thought maybe she was just going through a phase she would eventually come out of, but when it affected her sex drive to the point she went months refusing to let me touch her, I was back to thinking strictly of myself.

I started griping about how she was leaving me hanging, projecting suspicions onto her that there must've been another guy, and accusing her of being inconsiderate of my needs. The irony.

None of it worked. She continued being in every other mood but the one where she wanted to do anything physical with me. She was always too sleepy, stressed, or something else she used to describe the natural withdrawal her body made from me from knowing something wasn't right.

The truth is, her heart was aching, but all I could think about was my body craving sex. The more distant we grew, the more I added to the problem that created the distance in the first place; I engaged more and more with the side-situationship partners without the sex, and eventually added the sex.

Due to strings I kept attached months prior to, that end result was inevitable, but at this point, I fooled myself into thinking it was justified. As far as I was concerned, the relationship was going to end soon, anyway, I was just getting a head start, and it was possible she was too. I thought this would clear my mind of the sexual frustration and make it easier on me when the break-up happened, or best-case scenario, hold out long enough for her to come out of her funk, but the exact opposite took place.

My guilty conscience harassed me so badly I started looking for evidence that she cheated on me, too. Under normal circum-stances, it would've broken me, but under the ones I created, it offered vindication for my own transgressions. However, when I went looking, I came up with nothing, which tripled my guilt and added well-deserved shame.

The truth may set you free, but continuing to live a lie feels like making bail when you're at your lowest, and that's exactly what I did until she went looking for evidence that I cheated on her and found it.

When she approached me one morning to ask me, I answered with silence. My day had come, but without the courage to so much as dignify her with the answer she already knew, I just looked at her with confirmation and waited for what was next.

The emotionally heightened aftermath that you'd expect fol-lowed, and she didn't talk to me for a few days, then we sat down again, and I apologized and asked for another chance. Yes, I genuinely wanted another chance, but no, I did not deserve one and there's a huge difference. Me wanting another chance at that time was just me not wanting to accept the consequences of my actions.

It's amazing how you're only able to see the negative in something until it's almost gone, then you see it for what it was. It's like people who hate their life until there's a near-death experience, and that restores their appreciation for it. I had gotten so focused on the negatives of the relationship, I forgot what it was like before that, and what it would've been without me slowly deteriorating it over time, and now I wanted to keep it.

We had a good thing, even at that age. We encouraged each other through our lows and supported one another through our highs. We exchanged romantic gestures on occasion and made a big deal of the holidays I personally had never cared before we met. We had a friendship within the relationship, but somewhere along the way, we lost it. I blame myself for that, but there was no denying that we were no longer interacting as the friends we once were.

When I asked her for another chance, she paused for a while, and then agreed that she wanted to continue on, at least verbally. Her mouth said yes, but her heart couldn't take me back even if it wanted to.

We moved forward while being stuck in that moment at the same time. I could tell because she didn't look at me the same nor did she seem to look at herself the same. The best friend

I made a little over a year prior had been replaced with a complete stranger.

Her behavior became suspect. She began hanging out, not just all night but sometimes overnight. She started drinking and running with a group of girls who were nothing like those she'd hung out with before. Maybe she was cheating, maybe she wasn't, but either way, it was far outside of her character to be doing any of this, and despite several attempts to get her to let me know why she was acting this way, she wouldn't let me in. She blew me off or gave me some other abstract explanation that didn't add up.

Whether this was a justified retaliation, or just a good-girl-gone-bad situation, our environment became toxic and neither of us were benefitting from being in it anymore. The love was gone, and so was the health of our relationship.

I sat her down and asked what could be done to fix it. More time? More from me? I was willing to do anything and had already cut off and kept off the girls I had dealt with before, but it was clear the damage was already done. Neither of us knew the next step to healing, nor if it was even possible. So, we called it quits.

The truth was, she had unconditionally loved me, in action form, and with every day that she did, she loved herself less because deep down she knew she deserved better than the things I'd begun doing. She allowed herself to tolerate so much of my disrespect for the relationship that it ate at her original identity and nestled its way in as a part of what she taught herself was normal. Without condition, she continued to love me and it cost her herself, and that's when she became someone else.

As I was talking to Calvin, I realized this issue with unconditional love. It turns a woman's intuition off when it's telling her she's supposed to leave. It offers her denial when a man's actions say he's not doing any better than he was before the last time he apologized. It removes consequences of actions that don't align with words. It allows the line between imperfect and not worth it to blur because there's nothing to lose either way, at least not for the wrongdoer.

It's no coincidence that everything in life worth having comes with conditions. Ivy league students are conditionally allowed to remain enrolled by maintaining a minimum GPA. High-level employees conditionally keep their careers by meeting company standards and bringing tremendous value. Athletes are conditionally inducted into the Hall of Fame by performing at extremely high levels. Companies are only able to remain in the Fortune 500 by earning a certain level of revenue. A president can only remain president if he or she doesn't violate the conditions that would result in impeachment. With great power comes great responsibility, and with significant value comes high expectations to keep that value. So, why should someone be allowed to receive the love of another person without having to meet certain conditions?

Most people think of conditions in a relationship as things like financial situations, weight gain, rough patches, etc. But no, most of those things can be worked out and should not be held as deal breakers for love. Conditions like abuse, toxicity, and yes, infidelity should absolutely be conditions. If not for permanent loss of access to a person's love, then at least long enough for the wrongdoer to get themselves together and the victim to heal from the pain.

There's no healthy relationship today that's unconditional even if those in the relationship feel like it is. If two people have a healthy level of romance in their relationship after years of being together, it's because they're meeting the conditions necessary to fall in love over and over again. If a couple trusts each other wholeheartedly, that's because they've been effectively meeting the condition of transparency and honesty. If a couple gets into disagreements but remains respectful of each other no matter what, that's because conditions of anger management and patience are being met.

Conditions are like fire extinguishers. They're mere safety precautions that cause no harm to have around but will minimize the damage if things start going up in flames. If a woman gives her heart under the condition that he keep it whole, then a man who doesn't do things to break it will have nothing to worry about. If she promises to love him through thick and thin in terms of life's hardships, but still needs to be able to live without fear of physical harm, then a guy who's not abusive will have no issue with that. The only people that should have an issue with conditions like these in a relationship are those not ready to be in one.

My girlfriend's love didn't come with conditions. If it did, she would've hit the kill switch long before we got to the bitter end where so much damage had been done.

None of my excuses, apologies, or guarantees to do better going forward could heal her shattered heart. The only solution would have had to have been preventative, something in place from the beginning that would've stopped the destruction before it had gotten to that point. The solution would have been conditional love.

CHAPTER 3

How to Know She's Gone for Good

Treating a woman right and being right for that woman are two completely different things.

Yes, they're both important, but treating her right is what men tend to do when things are going great. When we're happy, satisfied, not distracted, our finances are good, our self-esteem is at its peak, and there are no drugs involved. It's like making a New Year's resolution and going to the gym. Your outfit is nice, you feel amazing, and you're motivated more than ever to take control of your health, so in that moment, you're looking, feeling, and acting like the champ you know you're capable of being.

But when the soreness kicks in, or after a few weeks when you don't see the results you thought you worked so hard to earn, or when you haven't been getting the same amount of rest lately because of work, or when you're stressed because of the bills, that's when the real you, or what I refer to as your default, surfaces and will produce the results you ultimately will have to live with.

Now my friend Calvin didn't give a damn about being a good man as far as relationships went, and his intentions were no good regardless of who he was with. He didn't see relationships as something to be necessarily good at, but rather another game to win, even in a relationship where he actually cared for the girl he was with. At least, where he thought he cared because about six months later we were right back at the round table dissecting another breakup, but this time it was his.

Back then, I wouldn't have dared calling the kettle black being that I had just gotten done being the pot, but a part of me knew he was headed nowhere fast with the first girl I'd ever heard him refer to as "special." By his standards, that meant something, and knowing him personally, I could tell that he honestly felt that way from seeing them up close from beginning to end.

During conversation, he'd keep his eyes locked into hers instead of letting them run down her curves and getting stuck while she asked him if he was still listening. He'd go on and on about how he was tired of the club life the same way she was and wanted to travel to some new places when he found "that one" to travel with him. Of course, he also had a side of him that, according to him, he didn't show to the rest of the world due to some experiences of opening up before and being shown just how cold people can be, but with this woman, it felt so "natural" to let that side of him surface which encouraged her to open up, let down her guard, and prove to her new potential love interest that his vulnerable side was in good hands.

She held off on getting sexual, like many girls do, just long enough to not consider herself "easy". Acting as the gentleman he portrayed himself to be, he didn't pressure her to do anything she didn't want to. But she did want to, and after it was done, things started getting interesting.

Suddenly, he was not as focused on moving forward like he once was, but instead focus shifted on keeping the blooming situationship steady while he continued to stall her out on making the relationship official. All the spontaneous trips he once told her he wanted to take to distant islands became a memory, the replies to texts became shorter, enthusiasm to see her diminished, and she had begun slipping further and further down on his priority list.

Phone conversations went from open-ended treks into each other's minds to obligatory, "What did you do today?" small talk ignitions followed by "Let me hit you back" conclusions shortly after. He did the bare minimum while she tried to remedy what she noticed was a downward spiraling romance by doing and giving even more, and when she got the courage to remind him that he was supposed to meet her halfway, she was met with guilt trips about how that was a burden to him usually in the form of him calling it "nagging" or characterizing it as her being unsupportive.

Calvin's story was the classic case of a guy who'd gotten comfortable with the fantasy that a woman would tolerate complacency forever just because she was all in on a long-term relationship from the beginning. He felt that because he wasn't doing anything drastically wrong, to her knowledge, she'd continue to dig deeper every time she felt that she couldn't take it anymore. He didn't overestimate her love because it was still there, but he certainly underestimated her resolve to accept that she'd done more than her part and leave when she realized she could no longer wait on him to do his. Why? That's what he was used to.

One would think that with such a good woman, he'd come to his senses sooner or later, but her being good had an adverse effect. The better she treated him and the harder she tried to keep him true to what he originally presented himself as, the more he fooled himself into thinking she'd never leave. To him it was evidence that she was in deep beyond her own control.

While I was no shiny star myself, I was puzzled when I noticed him blowing her off later on in the relationship, and when I asked him why, he nonchalantly explained that, "She ain't goin' nowhere," as if that was the green light to shutdown his efforts to keep her because the job was permanently done.

About a month and a few "Hey, how you been?" texts from him that were left on "read" later, the "She ain't goin' nowhere," turned into, "You think she gon' hit me back?" It started setting in on him that maybe he should've been different with this one. Maybe this one wasn't a game after all, or maybe he didn't know the rules as well as he thought he did.

His "care" for her, which I don't think he ever dignified as real love, began eating at his conscience when he realized he couldn't just backtrack his way into her space anymore after she'd created distance. She had completely cut him off, so it seemed, so he asked me what I thought for a little friendly reassurance.

I failed him, miserably. Based on the evidence, there was nothing I could give to foster that hope that she was coming back.

For starters, his sex game was trash. I wasn't in the bedrooms with them to witness, but boys talk (emphasis on *boys*). He told me how he only wanted head from her most nights because he was too lazy to get up and deliver. He also told me how he didn't give her head, even though she'd ask for it. He told me how he saw no point in trying to "make it last", when they did have sex because he got bored easily.

He was selfish in the bedroom, and although their relationship rightfully ended, it likely would've strung out longer and would stand a chance for another try if not for his sub-par efforts to make love to her. Why? Because good sex is like glue, while bad sex is like a chokehold. When a relationship ends, a woman is either going to feel like her body is still attached to her ex, or she's going to feel like she can finally breathe again, and judging by what he told me, I wouldn't have been surprised if she'd already found somebody to make her exhale…figuratively speaking.

Calvin's girl stayed with him as long as she did because it was about more than sex, and she figured she could tolerate the lack in that area with enough focus on the other areas. For a best friendship, underwhelming sex would've been a small price to pay. But when the friendship started feeling like acquaintances who lost touch more and more by the day, bad sex likely became intolerable. I wouldn't be surprised if towards the end of the relationship, she simply stopped asking for it altogether, so when being asked to return for a second chance, not only did the memory of their sex life not serve as an incentive, it was a deterrent.

The second reason I could not assure him his ex would ever talk to him again is because he'd made himself not just replaceable, but easily upgradeable. Sometimes men forget that complacency, inconsistency, and neglect comes at a price, and in the emerging era of Russell Wilson upgrades, it could be the opportunity of a lifetime for that backup quarterback to come off the bench and show what he's made of. Does this mean she kept a bench of potential backups during the relationship? Absolutely not. She didn't have to. Women walk past a bench of aspiring replacements every time they pump gas, go to work, hit the gym, or transfer groceries to the car in the parking lot with men offering helping hands that they didn't have to ask for. While she may not consider the talents of any of these men when she's happily taken, when she's dissatisfied in a relationship or even single, it opens a door for these men to bust in and shut the old occupant out for good, eventually. If she's a good woman, she'll keep all bench players out of the game until she's made the decision to move on, but that doesn't mean she didn't scout the talent that presented itself in the meantime.

This is why many women in relationships will play matchmaker with their single male coworker and single girlfriend who'd "look cute together." They know he's a catch, but since their net is currently occupied, they share the wealth with their friend.

Deep down, men know this, and so did Calvin, but ego makes us stupid. It blocks our vision of reality and clouds us with the fantasy that things don't require effort on our part, so no matter what we do, it'll always be there.

Humility, on the other hand, allows us to see you have to earn your blessings every day or else you lose them. Good health is a blessing, but if you don't get checkups and work out, you'll suffer the consequences. A nice car is a blessing, but if you don't maintain it or if you drive recklessly, you'll crash. The same concept applies to a relationship.

But the icing on the cake that he could no longer have and eat, too, was his ex's friend circle. They'd been pressuring her to leave him alone long before she finally accepted that she had no other choice, and when she did, they welcomed her back to the single life with open arms. Peer pressure in these cases can be a good thing to help keep us from being stupid.

The same way an animal is vulnerable, alone, but stronger in packs, is the same way we are, too, as humans. That's the reason men who seek to control a woman do so by trying to isolate her during the relationship so that when she thinks about leaving there will be no one there to reinforce those thoughts into action.

But when a woman has good friends around that she hasn't pushed away due to her toxic relationship, they're there for her during and especially after the relationship. They may even check in just to see if her ex has texted so they can extinguish any smoldering hope that maybe things could be different this time. They clear schedules for girl's night in to keep her spirits up, host breakup parties with sex toys to keep her stress-free, and may even have a few guy friends for when she's back in the mood to entertain.

A support system like this is like the cousin to high self-esteem. Even when circumstances are bleak, a woman's crown never falls too far from her head before friends help her replace it where it belongs.

Calvin's ex had that kind of friend circle, so that, plus my brutal honesty left him no hope at getting that one back. She was gone, for good.

CHAPTER 4

"Every Man Cheats"

Growth hurts, and that's why a lot of people don't do it. It's easy to have one belief and never challenge it. It's easy not to know an answer, and just make something up to fill in that blank. It's also easy to convince yourself that's what everybody else has done, too, so to ease the pressure on yourself to do something different.

Calvin and I begin to part ways when I realized he was going to be taking the easy route the rest of his life. We got along great, but most of our conversations were fruitless at best, and although the love was still there, I felt my personal goals and his trajectory were in two completely different directions, and I couldn't travel with both so I chose my goals.

I remember asking him to be my accountability partner to help me stay on track in steering clear of temptation after being caught up in my cheating. While my fidelity wasn't his responsibility, I figured that's what friends were for and was more than willing to do the same for him if he needed me to.

But, he had a different definition of what friends were for, and literally the same day we had that conversation, he was introducing me to a girl as his "friend who thinks she's cute."

As far as he was concerned, every guy cheated, and that was the way God intended it, so I needed to be more obedient to our higher power. Cheating, to him, was no less natural than waking up with morning breath or blinking every few seconds. It was the way we, as men, were designed.

But no, men are not designed or predestined to cheat. Most men have, in some way, in at least one relationship, whether physically or emotionally, cheated. While the same goes for many women as well, for men, it's more often the case since men aren't groomed to be monogamous from a young age the same way women are. Men don't have their value as a human or worthy relationship partner attached to how few partners they sleep with the same way women do. Men also aren't pressured to give tenth chances to their cheating wives when she can't stay away from other men's penises.

During childhood, boys are asked things like, "How many girl-friends ya got?" as their uncle grins proudly when the five-year-old holds up two fingers. At age thirteen, he'll get the "birds 'n' the bees" talk with more emphasis on wrapping it up than waiting until he's not only old enough, but serious about the girl he'll be sharing his first time with. By his senior year, if he's caught showing any kind of public display of affection with a girl, he'll be taunted by his peers for being "whipped" since PDA is an indication he's off limits to other girls. These experiences send a clear message to men during our developmental years that monogamy and manhood don't mix.

But to say men should be expected to cheat is to say our behavior can't be shaped despite what conditioning we underwent growing up. If a wild tiger can be taught more manners than your Golden Retriever, wouldn't you think a man's wild penis can undergo the same domestication?

The problem is, with lowered expectations come lower standards men are getting held to, which removes all incentive to change. That's why any notion remotely resembling, "All men cheat" is both untrue and infectious with the mentality a woman should just accept being cheated on as a condition of not dying alone and men should rid themselves of any shame should we do it.

Case in point: "It's ten times worse when a woman cheats because it hurts us men more." I heard this relationship tip a time or two and bought it until I saw up close and personal the things a woman goes through when she's cheated on. It's not ten times worse when a woman cheats, we just care ten times less when we do it because we believe that's what we're supposed to do.

The only thing that hurts us more is our ego because we see ourselves as too good to be cheated on, not correlative to everything we pour into a relationship, but by virtue of simply being a man. It's like when Jay Z said, "I was just fuckin' them girls, I was gon' get right back. But you don't get a man back like that." Those lyrics epitomize how many of us view our cheating versus anything a woman does that hurts our feelings, like leaving because we cheated.

We treat our cheating as if it's a stop we make to pick up a bagel on the way to work. Like it may make us a few minutes late but chalk it up as a one-time incident not worth firing us for. But let a woman cheat and we'll cry rivers of hypocrisy.

Anytime someone says, "It's worse when a woman cheats," they're really saying it's better when a man does, a man's pride is worth more, and he should be allowed to care less for the same crime. It's almost as if women aren't haunted afterwards with questions of how much intimacy she now shares with the man she's forgiven was the same intimacy he gave the other woman. As if a woman doesn't have to think twice before bragging on her relationship after being cheated on because she'll look like a fool to those who knew about it. As if a woman doesn't have to think about all the times she already made herself look foolish for bragging on her relationship before she found out what was going on.

A woman's cheating is worse to a man in the same way a college grad feels insulted when he's told to go fetch coffee on the first day of his internship. It doesn't suck because we see it as wrong, but because we see being cheated on as beneath us, and only us.

Yes, most of us have done it, but no, that's not an excuse to normalize it, or even worse, give ourselves exclusive privileges to do it. Being stupid for a moment doesn't require us to make stupidity a way of life. I've been stupid before, but I refused to accept it as a part of my identity, especially when I knew better.

I didn't have it all figured out at the time and still don't, but what I did know was that there was a simple solution to not being ready to be in a faithful and committed relationship which was to simply remain single. The consequences of winging it weren't worth it, and trying to incorporate unfair advantages in my favor as a fundamental element of the relationship wasn't my style either. At the bare minimum, I could operate from a place of honesty, regardless of my relationship status, and for a while I decided I wanted that to be "single."

I began the chapter of my life I call "Safe distance and safe sex." It's what I wanted, and as a single man with no rules to abide by, I felt there was no better time to have it.

But if I could go back in time and talk some sense into myself, I'd correct my thinking to understand that singleness is not the time to do what you want but to prepare for what you want so when it comes you'll be ready.

Even without knowing exactly what that was, it would've been better to just be by myself for a while and let the smoke clear. However, as human nature would have it, I threw Molotov cocktails at my personal life instead.

Initially, my goal wasn't to be with as many girls as possible, but for however many it happened to be, keep them all at an emotionally safe distance. No lies. No games. No relationship expectations. All I had was consistent sex to offer, and it was either take it or leave it. For several months, I went all out with those who took it, sleeping with any girl who shared a mutual attraction and had good hygiene, and that's when I learned something else; sex is way overrated.

Not lovemaking. That's the good stuff with all the kissing, touching, connecting emotionally, and holding each other afterwards. But just sex. The kind that rappers rapped about. What all the body hairless guys did in the movies. That stuff. Over-rated.

If you broke the "just sex" rules and made love, someone either got jealous or ended up hurt by having to be reminded of the rules and subsequently ghosted. So, one after another after another, it was the same thing, different faces.

Meet a cute girl, likely in a sexually charged environment like a nightclub or house party. Talk to her, make a physical compliment, and if she smiled, exchange numbers. On the first conversation, let her know my intentions, and if she didn't hang up immediately, schedule the sex. Whether it turned out to be good or bad, that was the end.

I can even remember talking myself through the sex like, "Check to see if the condom is still on because you don't know her. Pull out, too, just to be safe. Make it last. No, don't make it last, she's going to catch feelings. Who am I kidding? I'm probably the one who'll catch feelings. She says it belongs to me, but it doesn't. She'll be telling another guy that next weekend."

Not exactly the kind of self-talk I wanted to have every time I had intercourse, so I switched things up. I figured that maybe if I just got one girl to have sex with on the regular instead of just one-night stands and random hookups, it could work out better.

Wrong again.

Friends with benefits felt more like friends with bullshit. The conversations never went deeper than small talk per the boundaries we would agree on beforehand. There were a lot of dry laughs when her jokes weren't funny to me and a complete buzz-kill when I'd have to explain my jokes to her. Just like the random hookups, there was still sex with no feelings involved, except good sex too many times meant that feelings did get involved just to get shut down later, which of course, hurt.

When I was in a relationship, being a hoe seemed "lit" but, it was way overhyped. Sex without a real connection was a waste of time.

I then did what a lot of us do. I confused being frustrated and pissed off with casual sex as an indicator that I was a relationship-type of person, and therefore, I must have been relationship-ready, too.

So, with no commitment in my way, I saw no reason to sit idly by on my desire to feel that connection again. Maybe it wouldn't be quite the same as before, but just about anything would've been better than the monotony of entertaining strangers just to switch them out for a set of new strangers when one of us began getting comfortable.

Truth is, I liked "comfortable." I liked sex with feelings. I liked looking forward to a future instead of planning the exit from day one. I liked being able to trust and being able to be trusted, and all these things existed in one place--a relationship. So that's what I set course for.

CHAPTER 5

How to Lock a Man Down

"I can't lie, I was only dealing with you to make my ex jealous in hopes he'd realized what he had and want me back."

Yes, that was the response given to me when I respectfully tried to cut things off with a girl I had been dating for a few weeks. For now, let's call her Mary.

Mary didn't seem angry and it wasn't a heated discussion. No feelings seemed to be hurt by either of us at the end of her statement. I didn't want to mislead her, so I said what I said, but apparently, she didn't want to mislead me either. I was a rebound…attempt.

I didn't take what she said personally because in some way, we were both just a part of the bridge between where we were and where we would eventually end up, but I was intrigued enough to ask her more about that relationship she'd mentioned.

My ego was unscathed, but I was curious as to what kind of guy it took to make a woman go through such lengths to send him a message that required weeks, or what could've turned into months to deliver.

As if she'd started with "Dear Diary," the floodgates opened about how she was in a three-year serious relationship, all the things that qualified it as serious within that time frame, and most importantly how it felt forced after the first six months.

By "forced," I mean her tolerating being called out of her name on a daily basis, regular threats of abuse, forgiving him for not just cheating on multiple occasions to the point he stopped even trying to hide it, but being willing to overlook it in the future so long as he used protection and didn't fall in love with the women he cheated with, and finally begging him not to leave her when he said it was over.

Despite it all, there she was, trying to pull on his cold-hearted strings to get him back by dating me. She even came right out and asked for any tips I had on what could do the trick, I suppose as a parting gift.

Was she desperate? Clearly. But more specifically, she was damaged. In a way, we both were, but I supposed since we weren't trying to love one another, assisting in this small way was safe to do.

So, I decided to expunge every ounce of hope she had that she could make the man who was not only hell-bound on leaving her, but never qualified to have been in her life from the beginning, stay. There are no tricks, schemes, potions, gimmicks, or good behavior that could change that.

Yes, that should be obvious, but what makes it especially hard for women to accept is the connection they've always been taught to draw between them and a man's actions.

"She can't keep a man." "If she's so special, then how come no man has married her yet?" "But what are you doing to make him want to cheat?" "You are what you attract." This flawed mentality is nothing new, nor specific to just trying to make a man stay. So long as women accept being man's scapegoat for his wrongs, the longer women will also assume the role of a shepherd who's trying to keep his goat from getting away.

But, men aren't goats. We're grown, competent (well, some of us) adults who know exactly what we're doing when we see a woman who wants to be in our life, yet we still walk the other way. We may regret it later, but we don't need anyone to coax us into keeping something that we want, and due to wanting to be wanted so badly, a lot of women defer to denial for peace of mind because the truth is too painful to accept.

And that's what the girl across from me had been doing. When trying to look better, submit more, tolerate more, and suffer longer didn't assume control over his free will, she was left scraping the bottom of the barrel of what she thought would be tools in helping her retrieve a man that was never hers.

He was gone, and if he came back in the same condition that he left, it wouldn't be to love her. It'd be to simply have her. It would only be because he knew another man was about to partake in what was still owned by him, in his mind. That's the only reason any man could dog a woman out like he did, and then come running back with his tail wagging the moment he saw someone else trying to have a taste of his bone.

If he cared for her, he would've realized by that time how much damage he'd done and removed himself based on that alone. And if he had removed himself because of that, it wouldn't be the possibility of her being loved by someone else that would make him come back, it would be the fact that he had dealt with whatever part of him he blamed for his previous behavior, fought whatever demons he had been dealing with before, and was ready to love her, correctly.

Mothers who can't provide a healthy environment for their child sometimes give them up for adoption and later return to at least be in the child's life when they're in a better position, if that day ever comes. It may hurt to see the child go, but when the priority is the well-being of the child, they can remove their own selfish desires from the situation and act accordingly.

They don't go running back to get the child when they see the child prospering with another family, regardless of their readiness to be a good mom, unless there is some selfish motive like a child's wealth. But loving mothers, even if they're not exactly fit to be the best mother, will be grateful that child is in good hands instead of only focusing on the child being in theirs.

It's no different with men, myself included. I thought about why I didn't immediately go running back for Da'Naia the first moment I began missing her, and it was for that reason. While I saw the error in many of my ways, I had no interest in rushing back for a spot in her life until I was confident that the root cause of those ways was addressed, even if it meant losing her to another man. But after losing all hope, I was moving on to navigate shards of broken hearts I wasn't responsible for on the dating scene. Lucky me.

But in a "cup half full" kind of way, moments like this conversation were a small price to pay for being able to witness Mary take her first step in healing: acceptance. More than likely it was concession to what she already knew, and getting told this from a guy on his way out of her life was the last nail in the coffin since I had nothing to gain or lose from telling her the truth, so there was no doubt that it was.

We went our separate ways, and a few months later I saw her relationship status change online with a newly uploaded profile pic of her and some guy who seemed just as delighted to be with her as she was to be with him. I posted a comment of congrats, and she responded with an inbox message confirming that this one was everything she tried to force from her ex, who by the way, did come running back. Mary had finally cried her last tear over that guy, and because of that, eventually got the last laugh all the way to the altar with a man she's still married to till this day.

CHAPTER 6

❖

Don't Be a Hard Rock When You Really Are a Gem

The next woman I dated was a complete 180 of the first one. Let's call her Nia. She wasn't some broken shell of herself. In fact, she had likely been the one doing all the shelling. She had it going on both on paper, and in real life, and her tongue was as sharp as it was honest. Most guys would fool themselves into believing they could handle her, until it was time to. Only problem was, she tried to let them all… at once.

Our first real date wasn't until three weeks after meeting each other partly due to our busy schedules but mostly due to her full roster of dating partners that I had to wait in the waiting room behind to get my slot on her calendar. Up until then, there were just Facetime dates when she had spare time, and when the other guys were busy. Even text messages had a two- to three-business day wait on them to get a reply, but anytime we did converse, our vibe was automatic as if we'd known each other our entire lives.

But, when our date night finally came around, my excitement had waned. I didn't expect monogamy, but after weeks of do- ing more waiting than connecting, all roads led to our first date becoming our last. I would've been better off just cancelling but was mildly curious if it was going to be worth the patience.

One thing I could appreciate when the time came is how much of a professional dater she was. She arrived right on time down to the last second and must've had a glam squad prepare her to be red carpet-ready in a dress that fit like a glove and make up that was just as good as any YouTube tutorial I'd ever seen.

Our conversation through the night was great and the food was too, but I hadn't even swallowed my last bite before I was volunteering myself as tribute to her friend zone. The conclusion of our rendezvous couldn't come fast enough.

She laughed it off without asking for an explanation, then said, "Okay." I suppose there was some science she'd developed behind that simple response through her extensive dating experience, or maybe she was equally uninterested in going further, but so long as it was cordial, I was good.

I even told her I was more than willing to join her for a cup of coffee or quick bite on her lunch break should she find herself in my area because she wasn't a bad person. Pursuing her just felt more like trying to get to a concession stand during halftime of a NBA basketball game than courting.

To my surprise, she took me up on my offer a few days later. I couldn't believe she had the time that was so hard to come by before, but I take it the line for just friends was shorter.

We talked about the guys she had been entertaining, and I finally got around to just asking her why she was dating so many at once. I was curious if she really wanted a relationship, or did she just prefer food that was free, for her.

She said, "If someone stands out, then I'll pick one." So basically, if they didn't cut themselves off like I did, she would do it for the least impressive ones. But continuously accepting new dating partners to pile up on top of one another didn't make sense to me. Unless she planned to start pulling two-a-days or two-at-a-time dates, no one would ever really get picked. There's an almost infinite pool of bachelors for women like her, but last-man-standing style dating only works if there's a cutoff at some point so those potentials could battle it out until one had conquered them all.

For instance, when an employer is interviewing for an open position, yes, they want one applicant to stand out among the others, but ultimately, each person is going to be judged against a specific list of criteria, not just against one another.

If the only measuring stick is everyone else, and the door is open to everyone else, then the question of, "but what about the next one" never gets answered and it becomes a never-ending merry-go-round.

Because Nia didn't have anything in particular she was actually looking for outside of being impressed, her dating life was that same merry-go-round. A long game of, "Can you top that?"

She agreed that it didn't make sense, rambled on for a few more minutes, then finally drilled down to her real reason as to why she chose that method of sifting through men. It wasn't to increase her chances of finding the best match but because she was operating from a place of fear of finding her perfect match and investing herself into him beyond her safe levels. Thinning her attention among them all kept her from getting to that point of vulnerability and she'd developed this fear-reflex disguised as "choosing power."

Her explanation of this held a mirror to my own safety net I had not let go of before. The only difference was she had hers in her singleness, not in a relationship. Either way, as humans, our dependency on safety as a knee-jerk reaction to being hurt is natural, but when it comes to love or the pursuit of it, we must be willing to take a risk or else we're bound to lose before we even start.

She had taken the risk before and it ended in humiliating heart-break. A 10-year marriage that folded when she found explicit photos of her husband and his "homeboy" backed up to his iCloud that she had access to. Instead of moving forward with healing and an effective dating strategy, she resorted to one founded in her resentment for ever trying in the first place. One where she could have all the companionship she could stand without having to let anyone close enough again to hurt her like that.

I get it. We all want fool-proof ways to keep from getting hurt, disappointed, or blindsided, but the only way to guarantee we never lose is to also guarantee we'll never win. The same way you can't win at business without risking an investment, you can't win at love without risking disappointment. The solution is to stop gambling and start taking calculated risks by learning from the mistakes and acting on red flags sooner.

When I asked Nia about her marriage, she was able to recount every signal that led up to finally having those suspicions she'd suppressed confirmed. The times his friend seemed a little too defensive about disagreements she had with her husband. The times he rushed to reaffirm is sexuality even though she never questioned it. The activity on his social media where he was just "showing love" to men's photos that most heterosexual men would ignore. She noticed those things but ignored them, and in her embarrassment decided to throw those lessons away instead of using them going forward.

Her biggest hang-up was not the sexuality piece, it was the fact that his lover was hidden in plain sight. But regardless, putting a guard up so high that nobody could get in isn't a long-term solution, it's an indefinite forfeiture. People give the characterizations euphemisms like "savage," and "man-eater," but at the end of the day, if you ever truly believed in love, you can't just switch the programming of your heart to want something completely different. It wants what it wants, and it dies a little every day you starve it from the effort to try one more time.

For a second, let's think back to Nia's ex-husband, living in the closet, and all of those like him. Outside of the manipulation, deceit, and betrayals, a part of me feels glad that now he has no reason not to live in his truth.

He no longer must lie to himself and others about who he is and what or who he wants to love. There's a weight off his back that was making his day-to-day life a chore, just as with anyone else who is living a lie.

Nia is no different from a lot of people that are, in a sense, closet-lovers who pretend to enjoy the heartless, impenetrable shell they show to the world when really, they want a chance to be soft, vulnerable, and open with someone. But as a reaction to pain, they don't allow themselves that opportunity. They continue to pretend, essentially living a lie, except, instead of trying to fool everyone else, they hope to somehow fool themselves.

But it doesn't work. Fulfillment never happens, and neither does happiness no matter how well you're able to pretend or how much you're able to indulge. At some point, the thought of "what if" will come back to haunt you, and by the time it does, hopefully it won't be too late to find out.

Nia was understood on the possible consequences, but still not ready to face her fear. The good part is, she finally was able to see her fear for what it was instead of the power she'd disillusioned herself into thinking it was.

That discussion revealed something to me also, which was that if I never dealt with the fear I had, I'd end up in the same position. Sure, I was open to love at the moment, but if I was to come face to face with it once more, would I reach for the same safety net again? If not, what exactly would I do? Reach for something worse, just endure, or run? Before I found love again, I needed to find the answers to those questions. So, that's what I did.

CHAPTER 7

"Being Faithful Isn't Easy"

These conversations and epiphanies I was having began getting addictive. If you've ever felt that high of being confused about something for so long and then having it all make sense, then you know what I'm talking about. The more I felt it, the more I wanted it, and the Internet would turn out to be the best dealer, yet.

I binged on online reading material, ebooks, podcasts, Twitter feeds, and more that were geared towards relationships and personal growth. Some of it was helpful, if I could stay awake to make it to the good parts, but nothing was better than ongoing discussions where people were bouncing ideas and theories off each other.

I quickly saw that no matter where we're at on this planet, or what background we have, age we are, or ethnic group we belong to, a lot of us encounter the same issues when it comes to relationships.

One of the most commonly asked relationship questions everybody had was, "Why is it so hard for men to be faithful?"

I saw a person quote from Chris Rock when he said, "A man is only as faithful as his options." To Rock's credit, he's a comedian, so the context of this was probably a bit different than the very serious relationship dialogue that was taking place, but that comment had quite a bit of cosigners who agreed.

I wasn't one of them.

Figuratively, I get it. The more options, the harder it is. There's no way the grocery bagger at Kroger with a receding hairline and beer belly needs to have the same level of sexual discipline that a famous twenty-five-year-old NFL superstar has to have. New levels bring new devils, and the devils at the higher levels are probably a lot sexier and plentiful than those at the bottom.

But then the question becomes, if the man is still infatuated with having options on any level, then why did he ever make his choice?

Based strictly on my experience, the only answer to that question I came up with is that he either didn't know himself as well as he thought he did, or he didn't think he'd reach the level he eventually did. This of course, is given that he honestly intended to be faithful to begin with.

It's simple to write every cheating man off to the "wolf in sheep's clothing" category, and if I'm the woman in the situation, I wouldn't feel guilty for doing so. It'd keep me from getting taken advantage of due to believing he was a corrected misunderstanding away from being faithful and trying to wait for him to have whatever epiphany would make him settle down. It'd also allow me peace of mind as I created distance between myself and the cheater that I needed to heal from and possibly move on to someone who already had that figured out.

But regardless if I'm a woman or man who wants to avoid a cheater, being able to spot these deficiencies ahead of time could prevent me from getting involved, which is better than being left to pick up the pieces afterwards.

Of course, we know that a person can be deceitful and lie about their aspirations of being in a faithful relationship, but those lies are getting easier to spot the more sexually charged our society becomes because those people have less of the patience it takes to sell the lie long enough to cause real damage. One or two dates in, and 90 percent of "just here for the sex" types of cheaters are already unmasked and making their moves.

But the hardest part is walking away from someone who positioned themselves as a person having your best interest at heart, but still left it as broken as those who did not.

Spotting that person is harder because a lot of times, they haven't even spotted themselves, which makes all the things they do to get your guard down that much more convincing. If you're a person who being faithful comes easy to, it's going to be critical that you make the intentional effort to see the person for who they are because naturally, we tend to view people as having the same heart we do. And while cheating, one-night-stands, flirting with complete strangers, friends-with-benefits may be things you couldn't imagine doing in your wildest dreams, you would not represent the majority of people. Depending on a person's relationship vice, any of these things could be the warning sign that you need to tread carefully into a relationship with them, if not make a U-turn.

Some people's relationship vices are bad tempers, but we all get upset sometimes, right? Right. However, a pass on those small flare-ups or that person holding concerns in until everything hits the fan will result in apologies that can't clean up the mess that gets made, so it's best to address those things in the beginning.

For others, the vice may be complacency. But, we all get a little distracted or sidetracked sometimes. Yet, when a man or woman begins to give those excuses about why they've slacked off in an area they were once investing a lot of effort into, months, or even years will go by of one person being shorted of the things they need from the relationship to the point he or she no longer believes the word of the complacent one enough to stay. That could've been avoided by identifying the vice and henceforth, buckling down from the outset.

Cheating is no different, except our society is what cripples our gauge for what should be flashing warning signs that a person is playing with their own fire. We say things like, "Porn is a billion dollar industry, so everyone watches it." "Social media is not real life, so the same must go for the effects the hypersexual images and videos have on the brain." "There's nothing wrong with being friends with an ex." "Flirting is harmless." And we buy it. We treat those things as trivial preferences or personality traits, but for those with a cheating or sexual vice, they serve as roads casually traveled until he or she eventually arrives at the destination that wrecks everything.

The stakes get higher when he's not a loser with nothing to offer but headaches and a low credit score. When he believes in you, likes the same foods you do, and hasn't ruined his life like most of the guys who come your way looking for a free ride, it's not so easy to have these conversations and demand that he either answer hard questions about himself or come back when he's found those answers.

The fact he was patient enough to find out your middle name and ask about your upbringing was such a breath of fresh air that you forgot the most important step in getting to know each other is making sure he knows himself. If he's a stranger to himself or lying to himself, then what do you think he's going to do to you?

Maybe it won't be on purpose. But when your heart ends up on the floor, his dreams of being faithful won't do anything to piece it back together. It'll be too fragmented from the reality that he wasn't ready to hold it from the beginning.

You, considering yourself a pretty good person, especially with how easy it is for you to be faithful, will have recognized a good person in the man you let into your personal space. Because you thought that good in a general sense and "faithful" was a package deal, you forgot to check on whether those batteries came included.

Could he be a good man? Sure. But good men have their vices, weaknesses, and addictions, and if you don't have those checked at the door before you let him in your life, then that "good" man won't leave your heart in very good condition.

Imagine a room with just a table and on top of the table is a bottle of alcohol. You're told that all you must do is enter the room every day for two hours, for a month without drinking from the bottle, and if you do that, you can have whatever it is you want.

Whether you're good or bad, this should be a cakewalk. But if a person took this challenge who's a former, recovering, or current alcohol addict, things will get complicated, and more so if they've never identified their alcoholism as an issue.

Being in such close proximity with the beverage will generate curiosity about what kind it is, leading them to smell it. They won't smell it with any intention of actually drinking it. Of course not. They'll only smell it out of boredom, that's all. Nothing wrong with that.

But, the smell will trigger their pleasure senses, and disguised as innocent since it's not actually drinking from the bottle, will allow them to feel like another smell won't hurt, which, it won't. As a matter of fact, it will feel good. So good, it hooks them until it becomes a dependency the person now relies on to keep from actually drinking the alcohol being that a craving has been induced so intensely they feel like they can't help themselves if they don't smell it.

Depending on the person, how long it takes for them to go from smelling the drink, to licking the rim of the bottle, to gulping it until it's all gone, may vary but the ending is inevitable. And when that time comes, they'll recount all the things that make them a good person, and while those things they list vouch for their goodness at heart, it won't change that they were the wrong person for that challenge.

The connection here is not that cheaters deserve the same empathy as an alcohol addict but that as humans, our embedded inclination for error in judgment, particularly for places we're most vulnerable, should be taken into account before handing something so precious as our heart over to someone because that's what determines how faithful we will be, not how many options we have.

The alcohol addict type of lover may have been a cheater in their distant past or has cheated in every relationship but sincerely decided that they've come to a time in their lives where they're ready to be 100 percent monogamous. For that lover, keeping that promise doesn't simply consist of not drinking the alcohol, but also not smelling it, or even staring at it for too long.

However, in most relationships, many people justify those things as normal and sometimes their partner agrees so that they don't seem too insecure or distrusting.

But what people end up realizing the hard way is that the day comes when the love is difficult. One person gets pissed, someone must go out of town for a few weeks, a girlfriend or wife gets pregnant causing significant weight gain and mood changes, or a guy gets depressed so he's not acting like himself, and the willpower to resist our vice or previous addiction becomes weak. More times than not, this is where error in judgment takes place if we wait until we're already licking the rim of the bottle to try and not drink from it.

But sometimes a vice isn't born of a temptation that develops into an addiction. Sometimes it's a coping mechanism that supplemented a deficit in that person's life.

For instance, let's say the bottle of alcohol on the table is a stack of cash instead, ten thousand dollars to be exact, and the challenge was the same. Go into the room, stay for two hours, and not take any of the money.

For a person who's living in poverty, this money represents a solution to the deficit in their life. Although it would only be temporary and would cause the person to lose out on something much greater if they take from it, being in such close proximity to relief from the circumstances will be just as tempting as the alcohol to the addict even if the person is otherwise "good."

In a relationship, a person's deficit may be attention they never got as a child, the feeling of being desired they never felt as a pre-teen, or the need for feeling understood that went unmet their entire lives. That person may think a relationship will fill those voids, but when the relationship is no longer in the honeymoon phase, or things get rocky, they find themselves in the place of the person who's living in poverty with the task to keep themselves away from the stack of money on the table.

So now this unethical solution is more like a means for survival, even if only temporarily, and while some people can refrain, at first, from taking the stack of money, most will try and slip one $100 bill from the stack, thinking it shouldn't be a big deal because it's just one, and "nobody's perfect."

Just one phone call that gets accepted from an old flame that understood them the way they wish their current partner did, one conversation that goes too far with someone who's clearly attracted to them so they can bask in the feeling of being desired, or just one online dating profile used for flirting to stoke the flames of attention that have smoldered at home.

That small bill that gets slipped from the stack without being caught turns into another on the next instance they're faced to deal with the deficit in themselves, and as time goes on, it becomes a crutch that permanently supplements for purposes of coping, not healing. But few people realize that before getting caught stealing from the stack of money and forfeiting themselves from the challenge altogether.

I was no exception.

Looking for the answer to this question about why it seemed so difficult for men to be faithful helped me understand how I'd come into my only serious relationship with deficits, addictions, and everything else, and looked to a relationship to correct those things, and then outside of the relationship when it didn't. I'm grateful I stopped short of resulting to excuses, but without identifying the root, I never would've made the in-house renovations needed to change.

A man who's taken inventory on himself before he seriously pursues a woman solves that issue, not a man who has no options. A woman banking her unbroken heart on a lack of opportunities for her man to cheat instead of on a man who's done the work on himself so that no matter what opportunity there is to cheat, he doesn't pass on the opportunity to keep his commitment is setting herself up for failure.

A woman who requires a man to know how his past relationships, childhood, and broken relationships with his parents affected him doesn't guarantee success but drastically increases the chances. So does intentionally working towards a relationship with this mindset instead of just "going with the flow," and having the courage to recognize then stopping the indulgence of commonly ignored vices while still in their primitive stages.

Learning where I personally stood in this matrix of not cheating sounds unnecessarily complicated for someone who's never had the issue, but it unlocked emotional health I thought I'd never experience. Like going to seeing a chiropractor for a back pain that persisted for years and having it vanish after one visit, self-examining and tying up loose ends where strands dangled for years finally rid me of the chronic desire to have someone around who loved me and showed no signs of leaving. I didn't have to self-inflict the reopening of that wound anymore, looking for someone else to help me cope, and it was the most liberating feeling I'd ever experienced.

Unfortunately, out of sheer hatred for the act of betrayal, conversations blur the line of making excuses so much that we tend not to have them, which leave the work needed on ourselves undone. That results in history of dysfunction being repeated one generation after the next which has caused many women to conclude that, "once a cheater, always a cheater."

At first, I thought that narrative derived from women's misunderstanding of cheating, or everyone's misunderstanding for that reason, or simply not caring to understand at all. However, I grew to realize that most women who held this belief were taught this through firsthand experiences of being cheated on despite doing all of the things they were told would make a man faithful to them. They didn't nag. They submitted. They gave him no reason to think they were being unfaithful. They forgave the first few times. Then finally, they lost hope that any man had the capacity to change. It wasn't bitterness, it was deductive reasoning. "Once a cheater, always a cheater," had to be the correct answer because the other answer choices had proven false more times than they'd care to admit.

But no, cheaters are not ill-fated to eternal infidelity the same way that those who got cheated on are not destined for eternal naivety. Oversimplifying fidelity and infidels is cute for bragging about your morals and low tolerance for cheaters, but real strength is in recognizing the layers beneath the surfaces of both so that you can separate the real from the fake before you invest in a counterfeit.

CHAPTER 8

Narcissistic Red Flags

The more my experiences in dating conflicted with widely held beliefs, the more invested I became into the ongoing public dialogues around these beliefs. The issue was most of the conversations I came across dealt exclusively with relationships despite many of the issues in relationships linking directly to something that did or didn't happen during the dating phase. The most counterproductive debates treated the two as if they were one and the same, and it frustrated me to the point I no longer wanted to join these online discussions. I wanted to initiate them.

A few months in, I began receiving messages requesting my perspective on people's personal issues. Some dealing with dating, others with relationships, but to all of them, I politely apologized and declined to comment.

Why? Because only experts helped people, so I believed, and I was no expert. Yes, I was passionate about these topics due to the most painful events of my life being directly related to them, but I was still learning and a work-in-progress, myself. I was young, approaching my mid twenties, and I was nothing like any of the experts we traditionally see. Above all, I was deathly afraid of steering someone wrong.

But there was one guy who contacted me several times before I finally gave in and decided to at least hear him out. In a nutshell, he and his fianceé were on the brink of breaking up after being engaged for the past year and together for three. He was working unpredictable shifts with his jobs, which would cause him to be disengaged most of their dates, and he even sometimes canceled to go into work.

She didn't suspect him of cheating, but getting the short end of the stick on date nights, birthdays, or just quality time in general had worn her patience thin. He didn't know what else to do because she already knew he couldn't just quit his job, and he was working the job so they wouldn't go into the marriage broke. From his viewpoint, he was doing nothing wrong and she was being ungrateful.

I agreed that he wasn't doing anything wrong in terms of violating, but despite that, a woman can't pretend she's fulfilled in a relationship when she knows she isn't. I learned that firsthand under different circumstances.

Once I broke the trust in my relationship, it didn't matter how much of a fine line I walked, the trust was gone, and therefore the peace of mind was, too. So, technically, while I was doing nothing wrong in the moment I was trying to walk that fine line, it didn't matter because she still didn't feel what she needed to feel to be happy in a relationship with me.

I had permanently taken that away in my relationship, but there was still hope for this guy if he did what I failed to do before it was too late--acknowledge her feelings.

He knew exactly how he felt, but never once mentioned how she did, and if he didn't mention it to me, then chances were, he didn't mention them to her either. If he didn't mention them to her, then it's likely she felt like they were being ignored in which a relationship is all about trusting someone with your heart and therefore your feelings. But, you can't trust feelings to someone who has forgotten they exist. Without committing a violation, that had the same effect as if he had.

Solution? The next conversation needed to remind her of something that she not only forgot, but was getting drowned out by what his actions communicated--her feelings still mattered. He was doing the right thing, but even the right thing was having the wrong effect since it was constantly shooting down her hopes of seeing him, or even imposing on the time she was enjoying spending with him or taking him away from what little time they spent together.

He was by no means a bad guy, but she'd started feeling forgotten, and that feeling was making it hard to appreciate that he was still investing into the relationship but in a different way for the time being. I recommended that he remind her the value he still placed on being with her, make at least one tangible adjustment where time with her would not be compromised, and set a plan for getting a more consistent schedule that would allow for their quality time to not be so hard to come by.

He was the first person I officially offered advice to, and it wasn't strictly because of his persistence, but because I knew how it felt to have something slipping away that you felt helpless to grasp onto. He wasn't a lost cause like I was at the time, so I loaned him my 20/20 hindsight in hopes it could help.

And it did. A few weeks later, he circled back around to let me know that conversation saved their relationship. He still had the unpredictable schedule, but instead of giving her the excuses every time, he picked one night a week where his job would have to get the excuses if they tried to call him in because he turned his phone off and his attention on her.

A complete stranger trusted me to help him, and I delivered. From that point forward, there were no limitations valid enough to not help whoever would allow me to. I had the confirmation I needed that not only could I start discussions, I could provide real-life value on those topics that hit home for me, personally as well.

I began using my lunch breaks and time after work to sift through messages in my inbox, looking for scenarios I would shed light on. Some of them were pretty basic while others required me to take a step back and really think. There were some I wouldn't even touch, and instead referred them to immediately see a mental health professional or sometimes, the police.

But then I encountered a real-life case study of my own that I couldn't refer to someone else. Her name was Jasmine, a young lady I saw regularly when running my errands for work.

Our small talks when I came in to pay for my bottled water, gum, and full tank every week led to numbers being exchanged so we could talk more after she got off from her job at the gas station. I wasn't sure what it would lead to, if anything, but I was curious, and apparently, she was, too.

After a few conversations, I realized quickly that we didn't click as a potential couple, and I planned on letting her know sooner rather than later to keep things from becoming awkward, but before I could have the conversation with her, she had already stopped picking up my calls and responding to texts.

My first thought was that she clearly felt the same way I did and just beat me to the punch, but I noticed she had also gone ghost on her social media for the entire week. She hadn't blocked me nor did our last conversation end sourly, so I got curious as to what was going on and stopped by the gas station she worked at the next day.

Yes, I felt like a stalker, but at least seeing her would let me know it was nothing crazy going. But I didn't see her, and neither had her manager since before we last spoke. To his knowledge, she had quit.

Another week later I got a call from an unknown number, and it was her. What she told me next had me shook.

Her child's father found out we had been talking by way of one of her coworkers he had watching her. Yes, he had her coworkers spying. He knew about the day we exchanged numbers, and he knew she'd been talking to me on the phone by asking their two children about whether or not she'd been on the phone with anyone lately.

This had been causing friction between them after only the first few days, but she stood her ground. Not for us, but for herself since this wasn't the first time he'd been "monitoring" her and throwing a tantrum afterwards.

When she became what he considered "defiant," things took a plunge. He made up in his mind that her punishment would be him trying to ruin her. He went to her house and busted her windows so she couldn't stay there overnight. He also took her battery out of her car, which is why she couldn't get to work and eventually lost her job.

I'd heard of controlling men and women before, so I knew these types of people existed. What made me lose sleep after hearing her recount those events was that the entire time, she sounded as if she was rather unbothered by it all, as if this was a regular occurrence.

When I asked if it was, she confirmed it. Physical abuse. Hospital trips. Guns to her head. Miscarriages. Things you expect to see in a Lifetime movie, not actually hear about taking place in real life, or in her case, experiencing. She had no family to turn to because they all felt like she should just be grateful he was involved in his children's life and that she was being "rebellious" by not wanting to be with him anymore. So, her situation was virtually hopeless as far as she was concerned.

This might have been a great time to tell her something encouraging or inspirational, but I was already caught up in my emotions. It was too close to home, and the shock sent me in every direction mentally. I was enraged, sad, remorseful, and relieved that she'd survived him all at once.

My first thought was to defend her. Maybe I could be there next time he came by and set him straight. Maybe I could open my home to her until she got on her feet. I wanted to do so much, but none of it would've fixed the real issue. She had wounds that penetrated so deeply, anything I could do would be like Band-Aids to a broken arm. I knew this when she explained his behavior, not as proof that he was abusive, but in her eyes, as a byproduct of his love. This is what communicated love to her, because in her words, "My momma always told me that a man will only show that kind of emotion when he loves you."

I had to accept that this wasn't my fight. It was bigger than me. Getting directly involved would do more damage than repair since she wasn't ready to leave, and he wasn't ready to stop. This was a battle I could not bring myself to choose, so I didn't.

For the next few months, I wondered what could motivate a man to be so cruel. This was beyond just cheating. This went further than actions that didn't line up with promises. This was a monster, and what I found out was that most monsters like him belonged to a group called narcissists.

One definition of a narcissist is a person who has an excessive interest in or admiration of themselves, but that's like saying slavery was uncomfortable or Hitler was a difference-maker in people's lives. That definition is not just sugar-coated, it's damn near diabetic.

A better characterization of a narcissist is someone who not only thinks the world revolves around him or her but works to create that world no matter who they hurt in the process. All narcissists are not created equal. They range from the everyday conceded and self-absorbed pretty boy (or girl) to more extreme cases like the one Jasmine dealt with.

In the beginning, a narcissist will offer protection, companionship, or whatever makes him out to be an idealistic version of a dream guy, and once she's bought it, he shows his true colors. Except he doesn't just show them, he'll convince the woman she's the one who painted him that way, and if he's successful in doing so, he'll know he can get away with much more.

It all starts with things most people consider to be normal character flaws that you learn to see through or have patience with while the other person works on them. Little things like disagreements where he doesn't feel like he's wrong, so he stubbornly holds his ground. Times where he twists the things his woman says into something opposite of what she clearly meant, but instead of it being something he misunderstood, it's always something she miscommunicated.

As she continues to fall deeper for him, his dislike spreads to girlfriends of hers he doesn't too much care for without a legitimate reason, things she wears that communicate she has no respect for him if she doesn't wear something else. None of it seems like a big deal until the stubbornness turns into intimidation. The "miscommunication" on her part is flipped into somehow convincing her that she's crazy and doesn't actually remember what she said in the first place. The girlfriends of hers he doesn't like turns into girlfriends, male friends, or even some family members he has decided are no longer good for her to be around in which she'll have to make a choice between him and them. By this time, she'll be running on a treadmill of seemingly never-ending ways she needs to change herself to please him.

Except that ending is always a sad one, especially when you factor in the amount of time invested into trying to turn things around and any children involved. After she's worn all the right things, said the right things, stopped asking for answers to questions she already knew, and whatever else he'd demanded, she will have started to plead with him to at least try to meet her halfway.

Even with no faith that there is better for her to receive on the other side of the relationship, she'll decide she has no other choice but to leave. Initially he may not react to due to his confidence she'll come running back. But if she doesn't, he will take things to a level she'd not seen to make her life away from him a living hell until she comes back from feeling like she has no other choice.

Narcissists lack the capacity to empathize, which means that you can never expect them to realize the damage they're doing or to stop because of how it's affecting others. It'll be others that they're likely to blame for what they do in the first place. They will harass family and friends, turn the children against the other parent, try and damage their ex's reputation so no one wants to be associated with her, or at worst, resort to violence.

The "If I can't have you, no one can" mentality represents the worst of them, all. Nothing is off limits. Not threats of harm to both the victim or the new dating interest, using children as pawns, or even actual harm to whoever he feels like is a price he's willing to pay.

Listening to Jasmine tell me about things she'd gone through at the hands of this man she believed once loved her caused me to look deeper into the psychology of how that could happen. Both professionally, and personally, I felt a need to be able to make sense of it. How common was it? What was the cure? Most importantly, what were warning signs to spot early on so others could keep themselves from getting involved?

According to the largest study ever conducted on personality disorders, about 10 percent of the U.S. population is affected by narcissistic personality disorder, and disproportionately higher rates for men, which represent 70 percent of narcissists. I wouldn't be surprised if the total number of those who suffer from the disorder was higher since individuals like Jasmine's ex didn't seem likely to have sat down with any clinical psychologists to have themselves evaluated.

Nonetheless, while there may be no cure for the disorder, seeing red flags that a man you're dating may be a narcissist is as close to a vaccine as you'll get.

While most who suffer from NPD are great at fooling everyone into believing they're awesome people to be around, I've noticed some common threads in the experiences of those who've been involved with one, that would've spared them a lot of heartache had they not ignored them in the beginning.

For instance, if everyone loves him, that's not necessarily a red flag. But one way to see if there are hints of narcissism is to see how he responds when someone shows they do not like him. A confident man will measure whether it's worth his time and address it only on occasion. A man with a fragile ego may look to explain himself. But, a narc will retaliate every time, no matter how legitimate the objectivity.

Trying to rush into a relationship or having serious relationship conversations with a woman too soon are also red flags. Of course, it's no problem if he simply knows what he wants, but if he's identified a woman as his future wife after a few days when he doesn't even know her middle name, that's an issue. Men who are serious about settling down and have no interest in wasting time are still careful enough about their heart where they're not diving head first into something serious on the first date, but for narcissists to effectively "hook" their victims, they need the guard to be down. To get that guard down, they'll often shift into "I know you're the one for me," mode so the woman can give him access that she'd give to the one for her as well, and it's in this emotionally close proximity that he can do his damage. It also allows him to quickly sift through to only those most desperate for a relationship title who'll also be equally desperate to hold on to it once they get it.

Another red flag is a friend circle full of yes-men. Men and women all have habits or ways that need to improve, but if you notice he keeps friends around who praise his problematic behavior, then that's not an accident, it's a compliment to his problematic mindset.

If he goes out of his way to victimize himself no matter how at fault he is in every situation, that's also a red flag he's narcissistic. I remember when Jasmine would tell me about the things her child's father was doing to terrorize her, she could always follow with the ways she'd at some point did something to hurt him. As it turns out, he would always redirect the conversation of her concerns back to how she caused them, so it eventually trained her to think that way.

Are recognizing these signs a fool-proof method of avoiding all narcissists? In the same way that keeping your eyes on the road is not a fool-proof way to avoid getting in a car accident, no. But also, in the same way, it is a safety measure that will drastically reduce your risk of falling in love with one and trying to leave when it's too late.

Other safety measures include background checks, healing from your past relationship, accountability partners, or people you can trust to have your back that will notice when you're not acting like yourself. Your spiritual life, even if it's simply being aware of your own energy, so that when someone has come into your life that throws that off, you'll be keen to the alarm that goes off instead of mistaking it as just outside noise is another. Above all, the most critical facet of your preventative upkeep is your application of self-love.

CHAPTER 9

※

What Exactly Is 'Self-Love'?

The commonalities of the guys who turned out to be narcissists weren't nearly as glaring as the women who ended up being their victims. Those women, including Jasmine, were almost all women who had never thought much about self-love, or had an incorrect definition of it because they'd only ever been taught love for everyone else.

They knew how to love their child, boyfriends, and even their enemies, but no one ever told them about the importance of loving themselves. It was just expected to be returned as a reward for loving everyone else, so they thought.

But the problem came when they gave their love to someone who didn't give it back, and what that left them with. Even worse was when they gave someone their love, and that person returned it with betrayal, control, and manipulation.

With no other foundation for themselves but the relationships they built on the love they gave out, they hit rock bottom when they were shorted in return. This is why it's crucial to have a foundation of self-love, which is the understanding, acceptance, and protection of ourselves through daily actions and boundaries that get us closer to our healthiest potential.

We grow up being introduced to things that are supposed to fulfill us, but most of us are not asked what it is that uniquely inspires and engages us outside of whatever career we pursue. Our personality traits, things that hurt us, trigger us, who we're quickest to trust, what outlets give us the best peace of mind in the middle of life's storms, what body weight we feel the best at without any influence or validation from outsiders, are all things that really allow us to understand who we are. When we operate from a place of the answers to these questions as opposed to what we think we should be or who someone else wants us to be, only then can we truly accept ourselves.

Because we live in a world that doesn't cultivate individuality, acceptance is as much of a daily process as is understanding our ever-evolving selves. Putting those things that try and influence us towards the carbon copy of what is supposed to be our goal in its proper perspective makes a huge difference. The girls on TV may be beautiful, but that's not the only beauty that exists. It comes in your size, shape, and color, too. If you're a guy that sees other men on TV flashing materialistic possessions, that's fine. Maybe they worked hard for them, or maybe they didn't, but you don't need them to be happy, and anyone who really loves you won't need you to have them as a prerequisite for their love. The point is, you cannot fully accept yourself without getting out of the habit of comparing yourself to others, or if you're not mindful of what has access to your subconscious, that could result in you comparing yourself, even if you don't mean to.

Once you've grown to understand and accept yourself, you'd better believe that someone or something is coming to attack you. It may be peers or family who see in you what they wish they had, so they try and take it away. It may be a boyfriend or girlfriend who thinks that you're hard-headed or stuck-up due to the frustration of not being able to easily sway you. It may even be the long period that you have to be single before you meet the one you'll spend the rest of your life with that subtly makes you question whether or not you're doing something wrong and need to change yourself.

No matter what the case may be, protecting yourself is essentially the careful choosing of what battles to fight, and how long you fight them. Sometimes it means knowing when the one you're giving your heart to no longer deserves it. Other times it may mean limiting how many times you explain yourself for the same things over and over again. It could even mean walking away from battles you're invited to, when you're tempted to defend yourself against rumors from ex friends who hate the way others love you or lies from your ex once they can no longer have you but want to bait you into your emotions as long as they can. Even if you can win those battles, a part of growth is allocating your energy and time responsibly to things and people that deserve you, not just demand you.

Self-care is another means of protection. The same way stretching and strengthening muscles protects your body from injury, self-care protects you from stretching yourself too thin without the necessary rest and help you need to keep from crashing.

These days, there's this superhero syndrome where people try to take on life by themselves without help and without time to simply sit back and exhale but then wonder why they can't maintain healthy relationships.

It is okay to be tough; in fact, it is admirable. But don't let that cause you to feel any shame in allowing yourself some time to breathe, nor to feel weak because you don't always want to be strong. Sometimes life can be so tough and our environment unwelcoming to our needs that we put them on the back burner to make do without them. But untended to needs don't go away; they manifest into sicknesses, depression, or desperation for anyone who's there at the right time to convince us they're there to help. But with proper self-care, you don't get to that place of desperation, and instead can take whatever time you need to properly evaluate those knocking on the door of your energy or see your trusted therapist if that's what you need.

When you're protecting yourself from giving your heart to the wrong ones and mindful about what battles you fight regardless of which ones you're invited to, people can't toy with your happiness that you create without them, and you don't hit rock bottom when they no longer contribute to it.

When you accept yourself, you don't need anyone else to accept you, for you. You won't be easily enticed by someone who claims to love the real you because that love for the real you will already be there. It'll be something they can join you in doing or feel free to leave if they have no interest, but either way will be no loss to you that you must fear.

Understanding yourself enables you to guide the right one, when they come, in loving you. Without holding their hand, it allows you to handle those moments when misunderstandings arise with effective direction instead of unresolved emotion that can't be assuaged. For instance, if a boyfriend is truly trying to love his girlfriend, but says something to hurt her feelings, she needs to be able to articulate exactly what and why it hurt her. Communication from a place of understanding gives way for either effective action or accountability when there is no genuine effort to right the wrong.

But too many times, narcissists can feign ignorance, play mind games, toy with emotions, deplete self-esteem, and burn out the hearts of those who love them because self-love was never applied before meeting them.

Cuffing season turns into open season for those who are unprepared, but the application of self-love would make all the difference.

CHAPTER 10

"Men Love Confident Women"

You know the feeling you get when you see a ridiculous-ly huge sale going on at your favorite place to shop, but when you get there, you realize that it's only at participating locations and no location is participating within a 200-mile radius of you? After reading through hundreds of messages waiting for me in my inbox, I realized that's the feel-ing women get after being told the sexiest thing a woman can wear is her confidence just to also be told she's "stuck-up," "too independent," or "too difficult to deal with" when she wears it.

It's not that men don't love confident women, it's that we're using the words "men," "love," or "confident" loosely. I be-lieve a better way to describe it is that men do love a confident woman…that they can have. But the same goes for just about everything else.

If she's smart, that's great, so long as she's not so smart she can see through bullshit and prevent him from leveraging that to have access to her he hasn't earned. If she makes good money, that's a plus, unless she expects him to make good money, too, or won't give him any of hers even if he "needs" it. If she's purposely single at the moment, and confident that when she's ready to date again, she'll receive the man for her, that's admirable, unless it means that he also doesn't have a chance despite his best efforts to show her that he is the man for her. From there she can expect to be called names, guilt tripped, or even told she'll be single forever because of it.

At least those were the experiences of women that reached out to me after questioning the value of their "confidence" on the dating scene. If they weren't for everybody, and therefore didn't entertain just anybody, they had to thicken their skin because most men would retaliate or shame them as if they were doing something wrong by being selective.

However, what should be considered wrong is that so many women have given more time to men that didn't deserve it than they care to admit. Time that they can't get back, trust they had to take back, and a heart they had to put back together. What's wrong is when a man told his woman how pretty she was being her natural self just to lust over women who were the exact opposite. What's wrong is the years many women spend believing they should try toning themselves down so they don't run men off, just to waste their time with men they wish they'd run off after being a people pleaser got them nowhere. So, to make it right, these women make their confidence an inside job, as they should, but the guys they meet still have a problem.

I can understand the false advertisement of men's response to confident women throwing them off, but at the end of the day, no woman should be aiming to make every or even most men like her because it only takes one right man to love a woman. And if the confidence comes from a healthy place and is there for the right reasons, it won't be so difficult to wait for that one man either.

What happens when a woman has the capability of unwavering confidence but decided she'd rather have just any man than to feel good about herself while she waited for the right one? She becomes the, "pick me" type. The ones who are pressed to separate themselves from the other women who are doing all the things that men hate like being "too independent," "too opinionated,", and "stuck-up" so they can get chosen by any means necessary.

They adopt the "go along to get along" mentality. They call it, "not taking everything so seriously," but it only results in being taken for a joke and looking like a fool. They don't ask that the man be definitive about what he wants in the future because they're fine just seeing where things go. They have sex much sooner than they should, not because they only want sex, but because they believe it'll keep him from running away long enough to see that she also has a lot to offer in a real relationship, which, if she's unlucky, she'll get.

Without being bold enough to stop him from doing all the things that were out of pocket, he'll choose her as his favorite person to do those out-of-pocket things with. Something like that supervisor that everyone loves because he's the one that doesn't care about texting on the job, taking extended lunch breaks, or punching hours that employees never worked.

The "pick me" woman is that supervisor, and to her, she's winning because she now has her prize of the man she succeeded in not running away by having standards.

Except these types of guys don't just take an inch and stay there, they take miles, and this is why weak men will always love pick-me women. They start with occasional disrespect then advance to outright, trifling behavior, if not abuse. One or two instances of neglecting her feelings result in an entire relationship where they don't matter at all. By the time she realizes she's fallen in love by herself, it'll be too late for him to care and she'll be in too deep to simply walk away, at first. At least before pretending to be happy in public while enduring misery in private due to the shame she fears from everyone who bought into her fake happiness.

While waiting for the right one is difficult for women with standards, being picked is the downfall of the "pick me" woman. The guy who picks her will see no need for growth, have no consideration for her well-being, and blame her if she ever tries to change that because that's what attracted him to her in the first place.

I've read about these stories playing out countless times. I saw the women come in my comment sections barking at other women about how they better stop being so tough on guys in which some guys would then praise them for being "smart," just to see those same women in my inbox a few months later, privately admitting the fate of their naivety. But it's not naivety that causes women to take this route, it's impatience, and mistaking confidence as a "man" thing that somehow conflicts with femininity.

The same way many men were taught that emotions conflict without our masculinity, women are told that being bold, self-assured, and no-nonsense is something reserved for men. That resulted in generations of women who suppressed their natural inclinations to speak up when something didn't feel right, to hold back on challenging notions when something didn't sound right, and to take a backseat on certain decisions where they should've taken the lead. Should they tip-toe out of the box we've created for the "acceptable woman," attacks on their date-ability come from every direction, be it dating potentials, friends, family, and the like.

Those outer voices can't dictate your inner voice once you realize that knowing when to put your foot on the gas and when to let it off is a sweet science of all areas of life. As a parent, sometimes you must tell your child what to do regardless of what they think is right, but sometimes, you really do have to listen to them or take time to help them understand why you told them to do what it is you told them. As an employer, there will be times when you simply lay out a plan and expect it to get done regardless of any gripes or opinions about it, but getting feedback from your team and adjusting is still necessary in other instances. Athletes are expected to execute plays drawn up by their coach but depending on the situation, are also expected to improvise based on their judgment. Dating and relationships are the same way. A woman can be assertive enough to get exactly what she wants and nothing less while understanding how to not be so aggressive, she leaves no room for a man to fit into her life.

You can be confident enough to make eye contact, first with a guy you like, while allowing him to make the move after that. You can be confident that he will call you back when he gets ready, while being confident enough to know that if he takes too long, you'll lose interest and find someone who's more consistent with communication. In a relationship, you can be confident that your man is making the best decision, but also feel confident in your perspective enough to speak up when he seems to be disregarding your comfort level with that decision. Misunderstanding confidence is feeling like there are only two extremes that exist within it: low self-esteem or bulldozer who flattens any man in her path so there's no mistaking her as weak.

Sometimes, this misunderstanding is handed down from their elders, and although well-intentioned, advice from elders typically comes from their era of dating, which doesn't always fit well in the modern-day dating world.

CHAPTER 11

Our Grandparents' Advice

An old buddy of mine named Brandon from high school was in town one weekend to see some family of his and we met up at the gym to work out. As former athletes, that was our version of grabbing a few drinks.

In between sets, if one of us saw an attractive woman, we'd nudge the other to look and enjoy the discovery, you know, guy stuff.

Except Brandon stopped mid-set and just stared at one of the women. That wasn't our style so when I noticed, I snapped my head around, thinking that whatever had his attention had to be worth looking like a total creep so I might as well join him. But when I saw nothing out of the ordinary, I looked back at him confused and asked, "What's up?"

He stared for a few seconds longer before acknowledging me and replied, "Ah nothing. I thought I knew her."

I let it go for about fifteen minutes of realizing his energy had shifted. Before he saw that woman, we were talking, joking, and laughing, then the next thing you know, I was basically talking to myself with an occasional "Uh-huh" from him every now and then.

So, I asked, "You sure you good?"

He looked away for a second and then told me a story about him and a woman having sex from a few weeks prior. He had just met her, but he was drunk and she was all over him, so they went home and made lust. In the middle of the night she was climbing on top of him again, this time without protection, but he was still drunk and didn't fight it.

A few days before coming to see his family, she called him and told him that she'd just tested positive for herpes and that he also needed to get checked, which he did, but had not heard back from the clinic yet. While he didn't have any symptoms, he was still paranoid about the results coming back knowing that he had slept with her, unprotected.

A voice from behind us said, "Come on, don't sweat the small stuff."

We turned around and saw an older gentleman somewhere around the early- to mid-seventy-year-old range in a windbreaker suit I'm pretty sure I saw in Walmart. Mind you, this was the peak of the summer.

"Whether you got the herps or not, don't sweat it. Who really cares? You kids worry about the wrong things. Just live your life," he continued as he walked off.

We both broke out into laughter before I told Brandon, "Don't listen to him. You need to sweat this. At least, move more carefully out here."

He agreed, and I suppose it might have helped eased his mind a bit in the moment, but I couldn't help but wonder what kind of experiences the elderly man had to have to be so calm about my friend possibly having an STD he couldn't get rid of. I was always one to value advice from those older than me because wisdom is invaluable, but I learned on that day to put things in perspective, too.

That man was born in a time before STDs were invented. He may not even fully understand what they are and think they're just things you get from watching too much TV. Who knows?

What I did know was that he meant well, and in the context of just being happy no matter what, he was right, but as for the practicality of his perspective in today's world, it wouldn't be in anyone's best interest to "not sweat" health risks.

The same goes for relationship advice from our elders. I tend to upset most people when I speak on this topic because my perspective seemingly flies in the face of the love and adoration we have for our grandparents. We've all seen the viral sepia toned photos of teenagers from the '50s madly in love next to a present-day photo of that same couple just as in love as before but now full of grey hair, memories, and a bond that nothing through the ages could break, and we want that. Of course, we do. That's what happily ever after looks like, but the route they took to get there may no longer be available in today's world.

If we're being brutally honest, not all of our grandparents' relationships were "goals." Our grandmothers did a much better job of convincing themselves that everything was okay when it wasn't because there was no other choice, and our grandfathers had even less awareness of their emotional needs than men today. That means that many relationships were much less often built on love, trust, and fulfillment the way healthy ones are, but rather on tradition and familiarity at the expense of love, trust, and fulfillment.

I highly doubt that any family elder would knowingly lead their children into harm's way emotionally, but many family elders don't realize they've lived in harm's way for most of their life either.

Just think of how sunscreen was once unheard of, bicycle helmets were for wussies, and no one new tobacco caused cancer. All of these were based on primitive beliefs of what it meant to ensure one's well-being, and it's for that reason as opposed to ill-intent that we should all be objective when hearing out the perspective from those our senior.

Seventy-five years ago, simply having a stable job qualified a man for a wife. Never mind his emotional health, character, intelligence, or moral barometer. If he brought home the bacon, he was deserving of a wife to cook it for him, among other things.

But today, we know that a man isn't husband material if he's not compassionate, patient, trustworthy, and apt for fatherhood should a woman be interested in having children.

Decades ago, a woman was not expected to speak up when it came to decisions made on behalf of the family. Her sexual satisfaction, an afterthought. Her mental stability, not a priority.

We know, now, that those things can all make or break a relationship, and rightfully so, although most baby boomers don't typically view those things as priorities.

Our elders were taught that that a woman should have a man for validation, and that a man should have a woman to create his legacy and make life easier on him. You know, because she's "The prize." This was one I heard mostly reinforced in church, a place I spent a majority of my childhood and young adulthood, but as I got older, I questioned whether it was helping or hurting us today.

I'm aware of the intangible value a good woman brings into a man's life in terms of her ability to manifest his small plan into his wildest dreams and all the other ways that she increases a man's quality of life. But the phrase, "The woman is the prize", or more specifically, its implication made me wonder if the woman is the prize, then what does that make the man? Just the recipient? The winner?

If that's the case, it must also be the reason so many men feel like their job is done after they've caught their prize, whereas the role of a woman being the prize carries over into the relationship where she continues giving the value like the prize she is for the rest of her life.

I'm aware that a man has never been expected to do absolutely nothing in a relationship. Even in the early 1900s, a man was tasked with protecting and providing for his family the same way he is today, but is that really it?

Maybe a hundred years ago, a man would have to fight off grizzly bears when he was out chopping down wood to burn for the house's survival of winter, but in the twenty-first century, men are rarely called to battle for their woman's honor outside of a minor scuffle should another man try to hit on her. If there's an intruder in the middle of the night, sure, he is the one that would know to go check it out, but those situations only occur once in a blue moon.

So, a man's role as a protector is much more of giving a feeling of assurance that just in case there's a situation that calls for extra help, he's there, instead of a daily demand from him to protect his woman. That's like getting a guaranteed six-figure salary for a job you only show up to once every two or three years at most. If we're being honest, yes, that would be awesome, but no, that would not be fair to whoever it is cutting the check, and in this case, that'd be the woman.

The role of a provider requires a bit more, or at least it used to. But in our modern-day society, women aren't living on the streets or with their parents, waiting for a man who's financially stable to come and grant them the honor of being his wife so she can finally be provided for. In fact, there are many women who are making more than men they meet and don't even care for his financial contribution at all. There is also a growing number of women who are willing to split the financial responsibilities in half with their man, which is fine, but it cuts the man's role in half on top of not even being needed in the first place. So, in the average household, this leaves a man's role relegated to an occasional protector and half-provider.

Does this make him a bad man? Absolutely not. But compare this "job well done" to the woman's expectation of being a nurturer and stress reliever for her man, a healer when he's sick, a porn star no matter day or night despite many women rarely experiencing regular orgasms when they do have sex. She's also expected to be the supporter of his dreams, which often results in a halt on hers, his maid, cook, laundry doer, childbearer, etc. Does it sound like an even deal to you?

If you're afraid to answer because of the conviction of asking too much of men, then don't be. Men evening the playing field of also being a prize for a woman is actually a win-win since a properly loved woman upgrades the same way a man does.

Contrary to popular belief, it's 100 percent realistic for a man to match a woman's value by doing things like supporting her mentally in teaching her things she wouldn't have known without him, helping her develop better self-care habits, reminding her to focus on the positive when her world seems to be falling apart around her. This is especially helpful to women who are hard on themselves, the same way society is. He could not only financially contribute to the household needs and bills, but help her improve her spending and saving habits, or push her to reach small financial goals that add up over the long-term. He should be already supporting her dreams but also willing to sacrifice if need be, at least temporarily if necessary instead of that exclusively being her responsibility. He could be her peace, or even her relief from the things she's been doing consistently, just to remind her that she has help when she needs it, or even when she doesn't.

There are some things men can never do, like have a baby, but what we can do is involve ourselves as much as possible into the pregnancy with our wives or significant others. In fact, I believe that cheating is so much more rampant when the woman is pregnant because men don't look at pregnancy as something we're to be involved with from the very beginning.

Many of us believe men are just required to show up for the heartwarming maternal photos and when it's time to head to the delivery room. So, when the baby's arrival is preceded by nights of wanting sex but instead, being sent across town for specific snacks to satisfy the wife's cravings, we're left twiddling our thumbs about what to do, and too often do the wrong things.

But unfortunately, pregnancy as a co-responsibility isn't implied with the roles of protector and provider, so many men blame the woman when she doesn't show an unrealistic, super human ability to both grow an entire human in her stomach and not miss a beat with her husband's romantic expectations. The worst part is, some women have bought into this belief as well and will excuse their husbands for cheating on them in these times, at least outwardly.

I've noticed that these women suffer the same fate of those who end up struggling to pour love from an empty cup ten-plus years into a relationship they thought would be a dream come true. That's the common denominator of any long-term relationship where a man does only what society asks of men while his girlfriend or wife does the many things asked of a woman.

I'm not the first person to notice this. In fact, I've seen count-less women express these things via text message screenshots they've sent to me, and the responses from the men they were texting were almost always something to the effect of, "Stop being unrealistic."

But, for most of the things women were asking of their man, it seemed rather reasonable, to me. Be a provider, protect when needed, but also do some of the same things for her that he en-joyed so much when she did them for him. So, I don't think the struggle is in our capabilities, but in our mindsets transitioning from what was ingrained in us so deeply by traditional thought passed down from our elders.

So, if Granny, Grandpa, or anyone's advice isn't centered around your peace of mind, growth, and fullest potential, it's time to second guess it. Anything else is only going to lead to a relationship that feels like a living hell, which doesn't magically turn into heaven because you endure it for a really long time.

CHAPTER 12

❖

Recognizing a "Good" Man

You may have noticed that many of the topics we've covered so far have dealt with what a man can do better, and that's for several reasons. Firstly, I am a man and after taking a hard look in my own mirror, a majority of what I have to share is going to come from what I learned in that time. But also because the mantle of ethical responsibility has largely been placed on women when it comes to relationships. This recent shift in attention in how a man can improve added to the experiences of many women who've yet to come across a man who cares to improve may lead one to believe there are no men worth believing in at all.

But it's important not to let the grim reality of how bad it has gotten to jade us from the possibility of how amazing it can be. For one, pessimism never produces the best results. It wires our minds to expect and solely prepare for the worst the world has to offer, which leaves us unprepared to make the best of the good opportunities when they do come. Conversely, the fastest way to settle for what you know you deserve better than is to convince yourself that whatever comes your way is as good as it gets, so you might as well take it.

Imagine teaching a class where you no longer flunk students but let them pass on D's and F's because to you, they're all dumb. As cynical as it sounds, that's essentially what giving up on good men is, and that's what I hear when women say, "There are no more good men."

However, yes, there are. Often, we confuse "no good" with simply being incompatible, but there are, in fact, many good men, or at least those smart enough to realize nothing is worth the price of peace of mind.

For instance, cheating is stressful because hiding is stressful. Lying is stressful. Praying that God will be your accomplice in not letting the side-chick be pregnant is stressful. Deleting text messages, being nervous every time your woman says, "We need to talk", and regretting the pain you caused her when she realizes who you really are is stressful, and stress kills.

So, those men who value their life eventually realize that cheating, while providing a brief thrill, is a dead end, as opposed to the perks of being faithful that hardly no one ever talks about, like the ability to focus.

Trying to do too many things is the best way to fail at doing anything, that includes being an infidel while trying to pretend to be faithful. Multi-tasking is for unimportant, menial tasks that don't require much energy, not for the most complex beings in the universe, women.

Some men have tried to hack the system by getting a woman who's not her full self in some area, namely self-esteem like those who promise to "stay in their lane" because they're happy to simply be on someone's highway. But, that doesn't last long because feelings will develop, and so will her needs for more from the side-relationship, and if she doesn't get more, that's when she'll swerve into the lane of the "main" woman who's getting what she wants.

Now that man has to wake up to see his woman has unlocked his phone and read two months deep into text messages he forgot to delete because a DM from an unknown woman tipped her off. After going through this, one may decide to see what it feels like to try and be faithful instead.

As a woman, you may be may be asking yourself, "Okay, so if I just explained this to a man, would that make him change?" Unfortunately, the answer is no. Men aren't wired to learn by simply being explained to unless some experience has already aligned with the lesson being taught. Above all, men won't learn any lesson on changed behavior regardless of experience if we don't, first, have three things: vision, good sense, and an understanding of the difference between a change and an adjustment.

His vision is going to determine whether he can even recognize how his choices and lifestyle are getting in his own way. Without that, he won't give faithfulness a try because he literally won't see a reason to. He won't see how good the woman is he lost, no matter how good she was to him, and he won't see the consequences of his actions piling up in the form of drama that demands his attention away from his goals, year-round, mounting child support payments that are garnished from his check and the fulfillment of raising a family he'll never enjoy.

This is more reason it makes no sense for a woman to try and fix a man by being a better woman or even believing that she wasn't good enough to change him. You can't give a man too much to lose if he could never see what he had to begin with.

But his vision won't benefit him if he doesn't have the good sense to go with it. A blind bus driver will crash, but so will a bus driver with perfect vision yet no sense to stop at the red signs that read, 'STOP'.

There are men who are well-aware of what they have but are too dumb to know that they won't have it long if they keep messing up. This is tricky for the woman on the other side of actions that prove she is at minimum cared for, if not loved, but continues to endure actions that hurt her. She has to make a decision to walk away from good that isn't good enough, something most people struggle with until they've gotten fed up with being more than good enough while receiving less than in return.

If a man realizes he has a once-in-a-lifetime opportunity to be with an amazing woman and sense enough to know that he'd better step his game up if he wants to keep her, the only thing left is for him to know how to make an actual change as opposed to just an adjustment, as so many of us do.

Adjustments can mean that instead of no longer cheating, he cheats less often, less blatantly, or hides it more skillfully. One or two more boundaries keeps the peace, and that's good enough for him instead of stopping the behavior.

Without understanding how to change or what change is, this could be as good as it gets for a man who identified a need for changing and had all the incentive to in the world. And while some women decide to just settle for this because "nobody's perfect," only women that require actual change will receive the man who has in his mindset, core values, and emotional health, which produce the end result of permanently changed actions.

Remember, this is not so much about the catalyst being a worthy trigger, but rather where the man goes within himself to address the need for change once he's triggered. If he stops short at surface-level quick fixes to simply reduce the chances of repeating the fallout, the problem will persist and likely come up again. But if he's willing to dive deeper into the things that shape his every day thought process, how he identifies with environments he puts himself in, what he associates with his actions be it instant gratification or inevitable disaster, and areas of himself that need to heal, only then can he truly change.

He may accredit the woman for being the reason, which is endearing to hear, but the real cause of his internal change was the internal work he put in. Keeping that in perspective is not a knock on the woman or against the power of real love, but the key to not only correcting harmful behavior, but identifying if someone has before you get emotionally invested into them.

So, while it's not true that every man cheats, it is true that most will be refurbished by experience, which isn't a bad thing. A man who's never been in love, never lost in love, never been hurt before, or doesn't know the pain of hurting someone he cares for can't relate to a woman who has been through these things, and the understanding he'd lack about what his actions could possibly mean when tempting situations present themselves may be his undoing.

Think of a woman who's never been through anything. That doesn't mean something's wrong with her, but there's just a different kind of love that comes from a woman that didn't have it easy in her dating life but finds that man who's worth loving to give her love to, one more time. When she's been hurt before, she doesn't run out the moment things get difficult because she knows how it feels to be left hanging. When she's been broken before, she doesn't open up so easily, but once her loyalty is earned, it can't be bought or compromised because her value is too high due to her own experiences having to question people's loyalty.

Men are no different, in most cases. If you find one that works hard, it's because things were more difficult for him growing up than the average person. If you find one who's appreciative of all the little things, you can bet he knows what it's like to have lost something important. If you come across a guy who values relationships, more than likely, he's seen or experienced the feeling of taking one for granted.

You're probably thinking, "Yeah, yeah, I understand all that, but where are these good men who already have learned and "get it" then?" The answer is in the same place you are, among all the others who don't represent the best your demographic, gender, race, background, hair color, or whatever label means most to you has to offer. If you're a woman, then you can likely think of women you don't trust, who don't have the same values that you do, or respect themselves the same way that you do. Add that to the fact it's not about meeting a man who's simply "good" but rather someone who is right for you.

Are there more good women to choose from than there are good men? As it pertains to being relationship-ready, yes. But that's not a valid reason to write them off as if they don't exist, nor does it serve you, as a woman, to have that mindset, and neither would it for a man.

We often qualify women by their degrees, jobs, lack of baby daddy drama, or high credit scores, but many men have a hard time finding a woman who's simply not dating while damaged, shallow, or committed to her own toxic behavior because she doesn't see it for what it is. However, if he wants to eventually find a good woman who has taken time to heal, wants more from him than his money (if he has any), or is constantly working on being a better version of herself, he'll have to first believe that those women exist, and the same goes for women.

We stopped staying up late on Christmas Eve when we found out Santa wasn't real. We stopped skipping over the crack when we realized it wouldn't really wouldn't break our mama's back (well, some of us). The moment we've made up in our minds that something isn't real, we act accordingly. The problem is when that something is very real, we get stuck seeing everyone else acting accordingly and living happily ever after with the ones we're still ranting about doesn't exist.

So, to believe, or restore belief that good men do exist, a woman must know how to recognize one in which there are a few things she can look for, the first being how he responds to realizing her value. If he's threatened by it, tries to make her feel guilty about it, or doesn't acknowledge it, then she shouldn't give him the time of day. But if he's intrigued, turned on, or refreshed by it, he's likely a decent guy. It'll be a break from the norm of his disappointments, and something he wants to invest himself into; new planners for her busy schedule, scoping out affordable flights to travel with her, exercising patience instead of telling her she's wrong for the effort she requires. It'll be evident in his actions that he wanted a woman of quality to build with, not just a woman to cooperate so he could use her.

A good man also won't fault a woman for what she's been through. "It wasn't me." "I had nothing to do with that." "Leave the past in the past," is a signal that he doesn't want to hear about painful experiences that shaped the way she moved in relationships are mantras of weak men. Of course, no one wants to dwell in the past for purposes of simply being a buzz-kill, but if a man has the capacity to be a good husband one day, he's going to have to love that woman, including everything she's been through. He won't be responsible for healing her, but being a listening ear, and studying every inch of her heart, things she cares about, is afraid of, etc., better equips a man to love her.

Knowing she has been lied to before tells him not to get defensive when she asks questions. Knowing she's been sexually assaulted in her past communicates that he needs to be gentle and not assume she's comfortable without double checking when handling her. Knowing she's been used before lets him know depending on her financially should be an absolute last resort. Extra care goes to the places that have been hurt, not just dismissals so he doesn't have to deal with it.

Decent men also have a healthy view of manhood. Whether he's from the streets or prep school in Bel-Air, or wears rompers, or can do a one-handed pushup, if he defines his masculinity by trivial things instead of being fit to lead as well as humble enough to know when to follow, a chance for a healthy relationship is slim to none. I don't know a man alive who jumps at the opportunity to wash dishes, but if a man thinks it's beneath him to do so simply because he has testicles, even when his woman who otherwise takes care of those domestic things needs a break, he's not the guy any woman should try and build with. If he casually calls things "gay" that aren't hyper masculine, or talks over women, the time will come where he takes some toxic measure to reassert his "manliness" the moment he feels like it's been threatened. Listening to those cues during the first few conversations can help a woman weed out the future time wasters.

Another indication that he's a good man is if he has a clear vision for what he wants for the future. He'll ask questions to his woman that give him answers to see how she can fit into that future, and he'll already be taking steps towards those goals. Men who are only concerned enough to send "Wyd" texts aren't planning on a future with you. If he doesn't care about where your next career move is or how many children you want, it's because that phase of your life is irrelevant to his true intentions.

Men who look for time to spend doing activities that have no chance of immediately leading to sex should also be on a woman's potential "good man" radar. It's not because good men don't like sex, but because in the beginning, there's more ground to cover if the foundation is meant for something long-term. Just about every man gets an erection during the first hug if he's attracted to a woman, but men who want to get to know the woman and not just what's between her legs will not steer the energy towards that direction. His standards for the connection he wants to have with her are higher, so the level of self-control he exhibits will be, too.

More evidence of husband potential can be found in his response to when she's not in a good mood. It's easy to be suave and affectionate when a woman is feeling giddy, but what about when she's not? What about when she's not ready to talk the moment he is? Can she still call him later and talk then, or did she miss that bus because his ego is bruised? What about when she is irritable from work, and while she doesn't take it out on him, she's not so in the mood for his jokes as she normally would be? Does he get frustrated and cut the conversation short, or does he give her a chance to open up about whatever's bothering her first?

Men who care about a woman's mood are going to be concerned about her mental and emotional well-being just much as her physical. Men who consider anything less than Chic-Fil-A cashier cheerfulness to be "stressful" for him to deal with will pick and choose what to love about a woman depending on what serves him. Out the gate, he's a take and take more, instead of give and taking like relationships are supposed to be. This is the man a woman will come home to and tell about her day to be interrupted with his snores while he falls asleep. It's one thing to be alone, but to be with someone and have them mentally find the exit the moment you talk about things that are going on with you is colder than ice.

Knowing what to look for in a good man is the first part of believing he exists. It reduces the amount of time a woman spends sifting through pretenders and keeps her out of emotional rehab where good men don't look for their women.

The second, and most important part is opening the heart for love. Imagine being that good man, with the potential to be right for her, but no matter what you do, it's met with disbelief and cynicism. Imagine showing every sign of good intentions, actions, and integrity just to have it ignored for the possibility of what's wrong. Any woman that is committed to the belief that there is absolutely no more good men left on the dating scene will miss them, run them all away, or eventually lose the ones who were courageous enough to stick around at all.

But there are more Will Smiths than the one Jada got. Michelle Obama didn't grab the only Barack ever invented. There are still men who will worship the ground their woman walks on, but you won't get yours if you're laid up with Mr. Meantime.

It's convenient to entertain every cute guy that comes your way, and some would even call it "carefree", but being carefree can cost you dearly if you want one man who's going to be all for you. While there are exceptions to every rule, nobody wants somebody who's for everybody. Women don't, and neither do good men. If a woman has her plate full with time wasters, not even a good man can bring something to the table.

The reality for a good man is this: He knows his worth, and in this day and age, knows he's rare. I'm not talking about self-proclaimed good men who think they're special by virtue of basic adult accomplishments like graduating high school, having a job, and currently not in prison. But an actual good man you'd hope your son would grow up to be like will have gone through many of the things a good woman does, like giving himself to the wrong woman. As a natural and completely healthy response, he'll be more protective over himself going forward, which means he'll be looking to avoid these five types of women:

The Call Girl. If she's naturally sexy, that's fine, but his thinking will be that she obviously gets plenty of sexual attention as it is, so if she seems to be going the extra mile to call for even more, then his attention could never be enough to satisfy her.

The Serial Dater. A guy or two she may be entertaining at the time he meets her is one thing, but several men means she's looking to have men compete which more than likely means she's addicted to power. Women who are addicted to having the upper-hand are the first to go to war any time they feel like a man is trying to take that from her, and a good man comes to love, not fight.

The Open Wound. If a woman blurts out everything her exes have done to her on day one, it'll be a red flag that she's yet to heal from it and is looking for a savior more than a life partner. Yes, that conversation is warranted later down the road, but not knowing when the time is right shows she's yet to pick herself up and is only dating as a way to distract herself from the pain she never dealt with.

Sour Sally. If a woman is cynical, rude, or is already showing signs of disrespect, that will come off as a snobby personality or just the way she feels justified in dealing with men, which he won't tolerate because he knows he hasn't done anything to deserve that.

The Diva. He's going to be more than willing to pursue, but if she shows no interest, he's going to take it as such, or as a sign that she feels entitled to more effort on his part throughout the relationship. While most good men don't mind taking initiative, at minimum, they also like to be assured a woman is interested. Men like to know they're not just wasting their time, just like women. If it seems like it's going to be a teeth-pulling match just to know that a woman is feeling him, then it doesn't matter how beautiful, smart, or awesome she is, he will lose interest. The biggest mistake these women make is thinking because they're the ones being pursued, then they've already passed the bar, so there's nothing left for them to do but evaluate and enjoy the ride. However, while a good man may be intrigued enough to pursue, he's still evaluating what he's pursuing to decide whether it's worth eventually catching or not.

Most women have some characteristic of one of those women, but if he's really a good man, he'll be able to tell those who fit the toxic unhealthy description and those who don't. It's the balance or lack thereof that makes the difference.

Good women have men they like to avoid as well, but what has been more of a problem for women are the men they don't avoid in pursuit of their "type." Sure, as a woman, you should be with someone you're attracted to, but if you are pursuing the type of man that excites you more than the type that fulfills you, you may be avoiding the very one you're meant to spend the rest of your life with.

This is not about a moral obligation to choose a "good man" despite being disgusted by him. This is a fact check on the things you told yourself made you happy to see if they really have. A tall man may make you feel protected, but what about a tall man who's not protective, versus a short man who'll fight to the death in your honor? A guy who has good money would certainly provide some peace of mind, but if you had to choose between a well-off man who feels entitled due to his bank account or a man who's frugal but would give you his last if you ever needed it, who would it be?

The point is, your type has to be based on the right priorities per the type of relationship you want. If you just want someone for physical fun, run with the type that gets you horny. If you just want someone to show off online, then go with the type that has the stat sheet your friends will envy you for.

But if you're wanting your next relationship to be the real thing--a companionship, partnership, and spiritually connected and growth-oriented relationship--then your type has to prioritize his character above all. Since things that reveal his character won't immediately jump out during the first impression, it may require you getting to know the guy who doesn't visually impress you or immediately sweep you off your feet.

It's not exactly the sexiest thing you'll hear me tell you, but at a certain age, consistency is a lot sexier than broad shoulders and a six-pack. A mesmerizing smile is dreamy until you realize a lying tongue is behind it. At no point should you settle for a man you're repulsed by in any way, but another thing you should never compromise on are requirements to protect your heart. Be flexible on those qualities you enjoyed in your youth instead of continuing to be impressed and blinded by the same trinkets over and over again.

I'm aware that there are women who have mature priorities in things they look for in a man and still get hurt. Women who go on a few weeks of dates, and the moment their guard gets let down, in comes the guy they're with on some bullshit to hurt them and bring them back to square one.

In this case, most would suggest you're not evaluating the man long enough before letting down your guard, maybe even recommending the 90-Day Rule. But, if you've tried that and it still hasn't worked, there's a reason why.

CHAPTER 13

The 90-Day Rule's Oil Leak

The original title of this chapter was going to be, "The 90-Day Rule Is Bullshit", but that reflected more of my frustration with its misapplication than the truth. The truth is it's like an umbrella with holes in it: good concept, but useless without a few modifications.

So, remember the women referenced a few sentences ago that go on a few dates, let their guard down, and still gets disappointed? That disappointment turns into paranoia when she's confused as to how she did "everything right" and was still left to feel the burn of a woman who had no regard for her emotional safety from the beginning.

While there's nothing you can do to control how a man responds to dating you, the power is in your hands as to how what he does affects you. Steve Harvey understood this and introduced what we all know as the 90-Day Rule, essentially stating that if you wait at least ninety days before giving a man sex, that will cut out most who are only there for sex, preventing him from enjoying benefits he had not earned and saving you time otherwise wasted on a man that wasn't worth it.

But if the 90-Day Rule is ultimately to save women heartache, then it's missed the mark for those whose hearts can't be reached solely through their vagina, which would be about 95 percent of those applying this rule. Time spent, full access to a woman's schedule, revealed secrets, investment, interacting with a man's children or him interacting with hers, and many other things can be avenues to women's vulnerability. So, closing off the sex highway is nice, but what about the others?

I'll tell you. A woman goes into a relationship with a lock on her vagina but gives full access to her support for his dreams: a new project he needs help putting together and promoting, help getting in good with her network. That access to her resources makes her feel like they're a team, but then turns out, that's all he wanted, and she's left stranded with these high hopes while he's enjoying the free upgrade she gave him.

Another woman gives it a month or two before she accepts an invite to have their kids come together at a park and play, and when she sees him connecting with her child, she melts while her dream of a family materializes, just for him to realize later on that he never fell out of love with the biological mother of his children so he won't be conjoining families after all.

Another woman connects with a man's pain and reveals her deepest secrets, things that hurt her to even recount for storytelling, and giving that part of her to him, counts as an emotional investment. But if it's "too deep", it scares him away and leaves her feeling like he took a part of her with him.

My point is, the idea of the 90-Day Rule is solid; don't give a man sexual benefits he hasn't earned. But as opposed to an incentive program for longevity that leverages the postponement of intimacy, there needs to be a protection plan on your heart and every door that leads inside it.

This is bigger than just determining what a man does and does not deserve to have from you. This is about making it out of dead-end courtships unscathed, so you don't have to spend time licking wounds after every guy who doesn't work out.

Think about how protected you would be as football player if your coach sent you on the field with just your shoulder pads on. No helmet. No knee pads. No mouth-guard. Nothing. Just shoulder pads. You'd be just as safe as the women who go on the dating scene who say no to sex for ninety days and still say yes to being played all the same. Most times, if a man can get in another way, he'll unlock the entrance to her body before his ninety days is up anyway.

How do you know exactly what ways to safely shut a man out without having your guard up so high it pushes even the good ones away? It goes back to self-love, the part about taking time to understand yourself and set boundaries once you do. What kind of person are you? What makes you tick? What pulls at your heartstrings? Do you feel guilty for hearing someone's painful stories out without offering yourself to help? Do you subconsciously hold someone in higher regard after allowing them to call you at times of the day no one else can? Do you emotionally attach to those you cuddle with, have emotionally naked conversations with, or those whose friends and family you meet?

Those things aren't necessary to get to know a man, and if he's there with marathon intentions he won't be in a dead sprint for your heart anyway. Taking time to get on the inside will show him that you don't open up to just anyone, and make him feel more secure once he's in. You can have in-depth conversations without allowing him to see the wounds you're living with too soon. You can support his dreams without investing yourself into them. Encouraging words go a long way. You can call him back the next morning if he contacts you in the middle of the night, even if he is just wanting to talk. If he has a problem with your boundaries, then earning your heart simply isn't that important to him.

None of us look forward to going through the different levels of airport security. But we understand why it's so important and would rather fly than drive to our destination, so we deal with it. Above all, we know we don't have any other choice because airports don't give us one.

Not giving men an alternative other than respecting your emotional boundaries is one-half of erasing the paranoia that comes with dating. The other half is simply avoiding the major mistakes almost every woman makes in the beginning.

CHAPTER 14

❖

Mistakes Women Make on the First Few Dates

Remember the changes we talked about to modern-day dating compared to how it was in the 1950s for Grandma and Grandpa? How women are looking to be co-stars instead of just stand-in extras, and how men are human instead of just horny ATM machines? Well, mentally adjusting to this new age doesn't come without growing pains, especially for people with old school preferences in a new school system.

Say for instance, high-achieving women willing to work with a man if he's not currently the provider she'd prefer but can't seem to dodge men who are either threatened by her financial independence or looking for a free ride. Or intelligent, opinionated women who want a man able to take charge when necessary but struggle to find one who's not trying to run all over her because "real queens know how to submit." Don't forget, nurturers who have no problem being a man's peace but attract broken men looking for her to be an emotional mechanic.

If we're calling a spade a spade, we're officially in the age of the overqualified woman, where most have taken full advantage of the ability to do, think, and believe more for themselves and relatively bring more to a relationship. Meanwhile, men's societal position hasn't changed quite as much and neither has our idea of what we're to bring to a relationship.

That's created an imbalance where the average woman is having a difficult time choosing from what she's being presented while stomaching her nagging conviction that she deserves a lot more. Yet, with there being more eligible dating options for a man to choose from, women are allowing themselves to make mistakes they later regret in the effort to not get "left out" of those chosen, one of them being the ignoring of red flags.

When you've been single for years, and you have everything else you want, but a man, you start listening to what people who seemingly have what you want, suggest. Those suggestions tend to be along the lines of not having unrealistic expectations, not being too forward about relationship goals, etc. While it makes sense to some degree, what makes no sense is how women are treating stop signs like green lights and then surprised when they end up in ditches.

For instance, if a guy makes borderline offensive comments, stares at other women's bodies as they walk by, splits his attention between his text messages and the woman he's on a first date with, those should count as deal breakers. Not because he's committed one of the deadly sins, but because even these minor infractions snowball into an ice storm.

Offensive comments turn into blatant disrespect both verbally and physically. Wandering eyes lead to a wandering penis which could bring wandering STDs back home that find their way to an unsuspecting, faithful wife. Dividing attention with a woman on the very first date shows a lack of importance placed on giving full attention to the one who deserves it, and therefore results in a struggle later for his attention when he's giving most if not all of it to women outside of the relationship.

This is not to say that from a first date, forward, everything goes downhill but similar to a job interview, if he can't do the little things right in an effort to make a good first impression, history shows that those things won't improve over time.

But, in the beginning when a woman is not emotionally invested, she's more prone to blow those things off as insignificant because they feel that way to her. She's not going to get uptight about something that doesn't immediately offend her, and in the interest of humility, doesn't want to come off as a prude who's expecting perfection when she's not perfect either.

Once again, the ratio of eligible bachelors to eligible bachelorettes doesn't help. Many women feel the self-inflicted pressure to "make the cut" as opposed to the other way around for a man who approached her.

However, the funny thing about your heart is that regardless of what the playing field has to offer, if you allow someone to love you who's less than qualified, you will lose in the end. You don't win because you're simply not doing as bad as most, or because it could be worse. You win when you choose a winner, and winners, while imperfect, don't show red flags on in the initial dating stages. So, if he does, then it's wise to heed and act on them right then as opposed to waiting for the inevitable disappointment to multiply ten-fold.

Another avoidable mistake women make in the dating phase is not asking the right questions. Contrary to the belief that you should never mix business with pleasure, that's exactly what a healthy relationship is. It's a balance of both pleasure, in terms of personality compatibility, and business as it relates to life goals, financial responsibility, values, legacy that's created for children to inherit, etc.

So, when getting ready to do both business and pleasure with someone, hopefully for the rest of your life, you must set course for those things from the beginning. Yet, many women are either afraid to scare men off by touching on the business-related questions, or their subconscious auto-completes those questions with the answers she hopes are there based on what's shown up front, which results in too many of those questions never being asked.

The pleasure department is established up front with jokes he makes to prove he can make her laugh, great conversation to prove he can mentally stimulate her, and her two eyes that prove he's physically attractive. Nothing's wrong with that, so long as there's not too much time spent relishing in these things before business gets squared away as well, which is the buzz-kill we'd rather avoid, however foolishly so.

It's nice to know that you can have fun with someone, but when you're in it for more than just fun, you have to ask questions about their intentions over the long-term, if they intend to have more children, if any at all, how important marriage is to them, have they dealt with past traumas and issues of their childhood, what gender roles do they believe work best for a relationship, and more things of that nature.

Why? Because the relationship won't always be fun, and when it's not, business has to continue on as usual without the breaching of contracts. Happily-ever-after doesn't happen because two people laugh and have sex a lot, despite what the media tries to sell you. Those things certainly create the "happy" but "ever after" is credited to the business that doesn't get compromised. If not, the happiness will be the glue that strings together intermittent dysfunction, extreme highs and lows, and an on and off commitment while the hearts caught in the middle don't have the same switch.

Of all the business questions to ask, the most important is, "What do you do for growth?" I posed this suggestion in one of my videos as an alternative to "What do you do for fun?" and the feedback was exactly what I expected it to be. Comments like "That's too serious to ask early on," were everywhere, which is more evidence of women holding on to fear of running men off instead of prioritizing the protection of their emotional well-being.

Of course, this is not the question you ask a man as he's introducing himself to you, but on a first or second date when the small talk has run its course and the ice has been broken, this question would not ruin anything that wasn't already headed for ruin to begin with.

When asking what a man does for growth, you're not asking for a list of every woman he's slept with or how much money is in his bank account. You're not being intrusive or rude. You're opening the floor for him to speak on something he should be busting at the seams to talk about anyway. That's what happens when you're discovering things that make you grow. It feels like you've stumbled upon gems that few people know or would care to hear about, so when one opens the floor for you to talk about them, that's not offensive, it's exciting.

If a guy is reading a new book that has opened his mind in ways he never thought possible, that's something he'll enjoy talking about. If he's visiting places he's seen on TV his entire life just to realize the media didn't do them justice, that's something he'll be happy he got asked about. If he's found ways to increase his peace of mind, mental stability, or things that have helped him stay disciplined along his spiritual journey, these are all things that will excite him about the woman who's asking, not turn him off.

You know who this question of growth will turn off? The guy who not only has nothing that he does for personal growth, but the guy that doesn't intend to stick around long enough for you to see what evidence of that growth would be. You might as well be asking a car salesman to explain the specs of a vehicle that's not for sale. That will be a waste of his time, frustrating, and yes, a turn-off.

But this question is critical for women who are progressive, growing, and investing in themselves daily to get closer to their full potential. Because no matter how amazing the guy is on that first date, or in that first month, or even first year, if a woman is growing but he is not, she's headed for disappointment, or even worse, heartbreak. Her growth won't be appreciated, may be ignored, or possibly even discouraged. At worst, it could be something he feels threatened by and turns around on her as if she's wrong for her evolution. At best, it's something he'll simply have no interest in, and her growth will result in a widening distance between the two of them that she either feels guilty for, or has to make the decision to end the relationship because of, but not before exhausting herself on dragging her man along with her. Either way, all of it could've been avoided by simply gauging how important his growth on a personal level was to him.

Furthermore, when a man values growth, he also sees the importance of its role in a relationship as well. If he views himself as an ever-evolving human being that needs regular investment to stay healthy, he'll treat the relationship in the same manner with an open heart for concerns or needs of his woman that may change over time and the humility to sacrifice and adjust as need be.

But, if growth is something he deems pointless, he'll achieve whatever end goal he has in mind, and his efforts to remain physically and emotionally present will cease. He will give her whatever relationship title she wants, but once the work he's done to get to that point is over, so will be his actions to show that he still wants the relationship as bad as he did when he first introduced himself. So growth, as not only a conversational topic but also a must-have quality, should be established early on and revisited regularly throughout the relationship.

The third, and possibly biggest mistake women make on the first date is being impressed by his actions. This may come as a surprise to some, being that the phrase, "actions speak louder than words" is so popular, but since when do we listen to the loudest voice when anyone can yell? It's not about what speaks the loudest, it's about what speaks the truth, which is something only patterns will do.

Yes, it's nice if he is a complete gentleman in the beginning. It should be appreciated if he consistently texts and calls to see how your day is going. There's nothing wrong with showing gratitude for thoughtful gestures. In fact, you should. But as a woman, your patience to let his patterns speak over time is going to be your lie detector test his actions take for you to know if they're indicative of the real him or not.

If he's just on a "break" with his girlfriend and spending that time away from home to sexually vacation with you, then he'll have to make a move quickly before his "home" is no longer open for him to come back to. Therefore, he'll either get impatient and make a dive for what he really wants or just go ghost to see if you come chasing him so that things will then be on his terms.

In a more sexually inclined world than ever before, the amount of time a man is willing to invest for something strictly physical shrinks every day, so waiting a month or two should do the trick in ridding you of most guys who are just looking for their next penis cushion.

If he has anger issues, he may be able to hide them in the beginning, but after getting comfortable with you, uncomfortable situations will uncover them and give you the insight you need to know what else he's capable of before you learn that the hard way.

Time is the most valuable, yet underrated tool used in dating because nine times out ten, hindsight allows us to identify how using more of it would've saved us a lot of trouble. The problem is too many of us allow the fact that time is such a limited resource cause us to rush.

However, rushing and prematurely becoming vulnerable to someone who hasn't proven themselves wastes more time because it requires more time to undo the damage and heal the wounds from the time spent in it. Similar to driving a car, we often rush to save time, but getting speeding tickets, or even worse, in car wreck would cause us to reach our destination much slower, if at all. But when it comes to love, the interstate is full of road raging, drunk drivers who have their heads buried in their phones with no state troopers to sort out the chaos, so the last thing you want to do is be careless.

Is taking your time a fool-proof method of weeding out all the bad guys? Of course not, but neither is a resume to an employer. It is a way to see, over time, what he's most likely to do over the course of the relationship instead of getting blindsided because you wanted so badly to believe the love he showered you with those first two weeks were indicative of life you two could spend together.

Sometimes, it's not that a woman is easily impressed or is in a hurry to give her love to someone. The misinterpretation of the overwhelming excitement, strong connection, and perception that it's mutual early on can confuse those of us who believe in soul mates that we've finally found ours.

A soul mate is defined by some as a divinely chosen person you're to spend your life with. So, when things happen intensely and quickly, it's natural to believe that everything else will fall into place by the direct hand of the universe and all we have to do is fall with them.

Wrong. This is not to say that soul mates don't exist, but this is to call out the impracticality of that mindset not at least being coupled with some common sense that even if two people are perfectly matched, patience will be needed to build an effective foundation for a long-term run.

Sure, if you want to believe that there's only one human in this world that could ever be a fit for you, run with it, but don't get so high off the idea that you are naïve to the fact even perfect ingredients require time to bake for a dish to be made.

The tools and materials for your dream home will take time to put together. Dream careers take time to attain. Dream bodies take time to earn, if you do it naturally, and while you can surgically take a short cut if you please, Dr. Miami can't save you from your impatience when it comes to building a relationship with your dream guy.

That "love at first sight" belief is just lust and wishful thinking. Sometimes it's validated by the events that follow, but it never fully forms as love until both people have become best friends, got on the same page for their relationship future, and stuck to the plan.

Soul mates are two people who, even if divinely chosen for each other, consciously choose each other and the work it's going to take to make a healthy relationship last every day, every argument, every opportunity that presents itself to go against the promise to not hurt each other, every temptation to just give up on the relationship, and every mistake that hurts the other, including the work to make it right. I learned this lesson firsthand from my soul mate.

CHAPTER 15

❖

The Moment I Knew She Was the One

My nights-and-weekends hobby of leading discussions and responding to people's questions about love had quickly turned into a passion that consumed my thoughts daily. It caused me to be late to work, distracted at work, leaving work early, and that's if I made it to work at all. Stress began to come from every direction because my supervisor was starting to notice, which meant I would lose my job soon if I didn't stop. I could no longer answer every message that was being sent to me because my platforms had grown exponentially, and most of all, I had grown an antipathy for singleness that words couldn't describe.

My platforms occasionally served as confessionals for how little I cared for dating, an attack on "fall back games," and how much I did not fit into this trend of being a heartless savage. I felt readier for love the more I grew into the person I wanted to become but increasingly hopeless the more women I met. Not because of the women themselves. Honestly, several of them would've been a dream come true for most men, but no matter how great they were, not one was right for me.

I got sucked into a routine of meeting them, having our personalities click, occasionally going so far as being physical, and then one of us saving the other the trouble of having the, "Maybe this isn't working out" conversation because we could both feel that something was missing. I knew exactly what I wanted--a woman unafraid to hold a mirror to my flaws while actively working on her own, one who knew how to support without enabling, who practiced confidence while working to accept the things she was insecure about, a listener, a nurturer, and a partner. I wanted nothing more than what I brought to the table, and would accept nothing less, but I wasn't finding these traits in the women I came across, and the fact that most of them were otherwise amazing didn't help. It began feeling like maybe there wasn't one for me.

But I'd seen the consequences of marinating in these types of thoughts and how it could manifest into reality, so instead, I focused on the reality I wanted. I began writing "Dear Future Wife" passages, and figured I was either going to speak that into existence, or at least mentally escape the hopelessness long enough to sustain my sanity.

Looking back on it, it was hypocritical of me to be growing platforms that were pillars of hope for others all while starving for hope myself. I was encouraging people to continue seeking out their happily ever after in the modern-day dating world while feeling like my only chance for the love I desired would require me to be born in a previous generation. But I'd already helped thousands of men and women regain their faith in finding someone, which resulted in it happening for them. So even if I was a lost cause, I'm glad I didn't stop pouring into those with a fighting chance. Yet, I still yearned for a love of my own.

As I continued writing out the future wife excerpts, I noticed a recurring theme for who inspired the words. It wasn't a famous model or celebrity. It wasn't someone I manufactured in my mind that checked off the different boxes on my list of what made a woman my "type". No, it was a real person. It was my ex, Da'Naia.

We'd been in touch about as much as you would keep in touch with a distant relative. Happy Holiday and birthday wishes. Maybe a text message or two throughout the year to see if the other was alive. Just enough to show that we didn't hate each other, but plenty enough to create a boundary no feelings could inadvertently develop beyond.

She'd gotten a job in her field after graduation as did I. We were both doing okay for ourselves, living our separate lives, but it felt less separate the more I wrote about the wife I wanted because I couldn't do it without thinking about her.

I had officially become the guy that realized what he had once it was gone. I remembered how much we would laugh together. While there were other funny girls I came across, nobody's sense of humor was as compatible with mine as hers. Without saying a word, we could sit in a room, send a joke to each other by mere eye contact, and on the drive home, laugh hysterically about it as if it'd just happened.

I thought back to how inspired I felt to achieve more because of the life she spoke into me, and while there were supportive women I met after her, there was a specific tone and message she somehow knew I needed in every moment I needed it. She could be soft without coddling me and stern without being insensitive. I'd considered myself self-motivated from a young age, but with her, it was more, and because of her, I was better.

On paper, there were other women I had met who had similar qualities, but when you love someone, all the qualities in the world aren't good enough without them coming in that one person. It took a while, but I finally had come back around to admitting that.

So, I made up my mind that I had to get her back, or at least try.

I considered what kinds of poems would be eloquent enough to convey my desire. Maybe I could dip into my 401k, get an expensive necklace which could earn a lot of cool points being that I never bought expensive things, then show up at her job with a lot of flowers to let her know how I wanted out of this not-even-a-friend zone we'd relegated to.

But she wasn't the type to be impressed by any of that. She was a put-up–or-shut-up type of girl, and that's what it would take for me to convince her I was seriously wanting and worthy of another run at a relationship with her, and that was if she would even be open to evaluating me for being worth her time to consider.

So, I just called her.

She sounded surprised when she answered, or more so perplexed as to why I was calling, since this was out of our norm.

But it was too late, and I was too deep in to turn around, so I eased my way into the conversation with small talk before cutting to the part where I'd been thinking about her, preparing for her, and didn't want to go another day without a chance to prove it.

She was silent for a few seconds before letting out an ambiguous, "Umm...wow."

I'm not sure if it was my nervousness or feeling so stupid at that point there was nowhere to go but up, but I continued in reiteration that I was well-aware of what happened before and that she may have already moved on. But if she was available and even open to the idea, I was ready. Whatever time she needed, whatever space she needed while she evaluated me would be fine. But I had to make it clear where I stood, and with her permission, was ready to pursue her again.

She said yes and agreed. I know, the way I went about this may seem overly "official," and it may have been more organic to just gradually ease my way back with daily small talk until the conversation came up on its own, but because of our history, there would be no tiptoeing into this territory. I had to put all my cards on the table, and fortunately, it worked out.

I was somewhat surprised a guy didn't already have dibs on that spot I was asking for, but there was no time for that. It was time to make clear to any woman who could remotely believe I had interest in her to now be clear that I was off the market. The last thing I wanted was to have a comment show up on my Facebook wall inviting me to something, or a call come in when

I least expected it in the middle of the night giving her the impression that I was still on the scene. No, we were not exclusive, yet, but I wasn't taking any chances. This was too important.

Once you know what you want, the other things you could still have don't matter anymore. There was no longer a desire for a safety net. I didn't need a plan B. This was plan A through Z and if it didn't work, I'd create a few more letters to keep trying until it did.

Of course, if she at any point shut me down, I'd have to accept it, but my thinking was that this was my opportunity, and I would go all in. I'd sacrifice as needed, adjust, and remove anything that would obstruct the space in my life she'd need both externally and internally, although for the most part I'd done much of the internal work.

Granted, I did it late, which in most cases ends up being too late. Being that we were only teenagers when we met, it took longer for her to go through her moving-on stages, but most guys in my position who genuinely learned from their past and became a better man after being trash in a relationship aren't afforded that kind of time to get it together.

An old acquaintance of mine from high school, who knew, on the surface, what had gone on in my relationship with Da'Naia and I back in the day, reached out when he found himself walking in my shoes. He had a woman he'd met, wasn't prepared for, and didn't take care of when he was with her and was now looking to get her back after realizing where he messed up.

I listened to him tell me about what he had been currently doing to better himself and I empathized because I, too, had been renovating myself and could tell he was ready to not only get her back but also keep her, the right way.

In fact, I was excited for him until he told me details about how things fell apart and more specifically, the timeline of it all happening. At that point, I knew his hopes were in vain. Yes, he had come to his senses, which was great, but he'd also allowed her to complete the Five Phases of No Return.

CHAPTER 16

The Five Phases of No Return

This doesn't apply to young or inexperienced women, but for those who've been in any serious relationship where they've played the fool, there are phases that begin the moment dysfunction enters the relationship, which act as a countdown until that woman is gone for good.

The wrongdoer simultaneously goes through his or her own five phases of opportunity to salvage the relationship, but with no way of knowing exactly how long each phase is going to last, it's easy to overestimate the amount of time you have to stop the downward spiral before it's all over.

Phase one is the Comfort Phase. This is where the one who's doing wrong gets comfortable in their wrongdoing and feels like they've found their sweet spot, regardless of what rules they're breaking or how it's making their partner feel. For some, it's casual disrespect. For others, it's infidelity. For extreme cases, it could be some form of abuse or manipulation. Whatever the case, this is pretty much the quiet before the storm, and then the storm, a.k.a. the breakup, happens which brings on phase two: the Single Phase.

The Single Phase is also enjoyed by the one who did the wrong. In this case it was my old friend, and he went on like many of us do after a relationship enjoying lustful freedoms he formerly had to work to keep hidden. What used to be covered up by phones being face down, excuses and alibis for being out late, or lies when caught red-handed now could be completely out in the open, paranoia-free for him to indulge in, kind of how T-Pain described in his song, "I'm Sprung". He felt free, released from the chains of monogamy, just to be brought back down to reality a few weeks later when he realized that she is, too, and that commenced phase three: the Investigative Phase.

In the Investigative Phase, he'd tried to track her new movements, looking over her social media for context clues, even looking at her friend's pages to see if they'd put any passive-aggressive hints about where their newly single friend was at mentally. When he couldn't find anything there, he sent text messages and called her to check and see how she was doing in which he really was just searching for a gauge on how long it was going to take her to come running back. Even if it wasn't in the near future, confirmation that she was going to come back eventually would've allowed enough peace of mind to enjoy the Single Phase a little longer, but when she didn't allow any contact and there was nothing to give him the assurance he was looking for, that brought on phase four: the Fight Phase.

He fought for another chance with everything he had. He left thoughtful letters on her doorstep, he professed his transgressions publicly on his social media to show her he was apologetic. He even begged for help from her mom, in which she gave him some words of encouragement before cutting the conversation short. He'd tried everything in the book to get her to remember what they once had, and more importantly believe in it again, but after a few months realized that it wasn't working. This realization initiated the final phase, for him, where he'd reached out to me: the Heartbreak Phase.

In this phase, a man's world feels like it's crashing down. Nothing feels right, nothing is enjoyable, we may even pick up an unhealthy habit or two trying to cope because we realize just how badly we've messed up. It's beyond ego, and it's literally a daily beating our heart takes with every memory of every action that had led to that point, and how none of it was worth losing the woman we were with. Some guys handle this phase by committing to a life-long journey of being a player as a way of keeping their hopes from getting up for truelove again. Some of us begin rebuilding our broken selves in hope for one more try, in which I felt like he was more than ready for, except it would likely be with another woman.

The one he wanted had gone through all five phases on her end as well, except in the reverse order.

Her Heartbreak Phase was in the beginning of the relationship when she saw the changes in his behavior from when they first met and wondered what caused those changes but kept it to herself. She'd held in how she felt, hoping she was thinking too much into it, but deep down, she knew something wasn't right and it hurt her to the point those around her could tell by the way her happiness left and energy shifted.

Once she stopped denying it, she began her Fight Phase, thinking she could keep the relationship together by changing things about herself that he'd like. Different hair, better sex, more food, less talking when he came home from work, less requests for things she wanted from him so she didn't stress him, etc. She fought first with herself, thinking it was something she was doing wrong, or maybe could do better, but when it seemed to only make the problem worse, which it really didn't, he'd just gotten even more comfortable in his wrongdoing because of how he interpreted the things she was doing, she went into the Investigative Phase.

She prepared dinner and asked that they talk. When she did, he avoided the questions, switched the subject, and brushed her off until it was time for bed. When she brought it up later on multiple occasions, it was never a good enough time to talk about it. He thought he could just discourage her curiosity, but he only stoked the flame more to the point that nothing was off limits. She went through his phone, social media, had friends spying on him when he went out, spied on him herself a few times.

This is where many people say, "If you go looking for dirt, you're gonna find it," and she did. While some women decide to go mud sliding, and excuse the dirt they found because they shouldn't have gone looking for it in the first place, a mature woman with her sense of self intact won't take that route. After being on the giving end of forgiveness too many times before, she's done.

So, this is where she finally reached her Single Phase. Not just physically, but emotionally. She had already grieved for most of the relationship, and having her suspicions validated was the confirmation she needed to give her closure with moving on to restore what she'd lost: her happiness, peace of mind, and focus.

But the final nail in the coffin of my old friend's hopes that maybe there was still a chance was not her bounce back to her old self, but the fact there was a new man in her life helping her soar.

Some people think it's just the mere presence of a good man swooping in to block the old guy out of the picture, but it's all in what preceded the new man that makes the difference. If she had not properly healed, she could've chosen just anyone, and that old thing that wanted her back may have looked like an opportunity she couldn't miss out on. But with her becoming whole again, first, this new man had to come correct, because she wasn't aching for someone to save her from the inescapable pain of a failed relationship. She'd already saved herself. She wasn't desperate, and she was wiser than before.

So even though my friend had gotten his act together, the role he'd once played had already been filled in by someone that met higher standards of evaluation than even he had originally met. Because she'd been naïve before, she trusted her judgment more this time which conversely meant she trusted the conclusion she'd come to about her ex and why he should not be allowed into her future.

Because she had no contact with him afterwards, her idea of him was frozen in the space of the time things ended, and at the time he wanted to change that idea, she had no desire, or even room to entertain the thought to give him a chance to reignite the desire.

This is why some men lose out on who would've been their soul mate.

I'm in the small group that's lucky enough to not have so completely burned the bridge with my ex that she wouldn't allow contact, and with our youth, we both afforded each other room for growth as opposed to indefinite condemnation.

But when a man ruins a good thing with a grown woman who was all in during the relationship and completely heals afterwards, his chances are slim to none of getting her back. Actually, they're in the negatives if someone better has come along to appreciate what he didn't, and that's exactly what I told my old friend.

CHAPTER 17

❖

"Men Are Simple Creatures."

"Why do men have everything they say they want in a woman but still hurt her?" a woman stood up and asked me.

I'd just finished giving a nerve-racking presentation in front of a crowd of about sixty or so people at one of my very first book signings. I always had a morbid fear of public speaking, but it's nearly impossible to avoid it per the career path I chose, and I'd already quit my day job with no backup plan, so there I was.

Her question mentally took me out of that conference room and into the time where I was exactly the kind of guy she was asking me to explain to her.

I began addressing various circumstances that would have resulted in her man taking her good qualities for granted, including those I could personally relate to. Maybe it was the time in his life, his childhood traumas, his immaturity, or maybe he was just lying to her from the beginning.

No matter the scenario, the man and his promise he didn't keep was the common denominator, and therefore the blame, but the more I spoke, the more I felt the glaring contradiction between the reality so many women faced and our general summation of men being "simple creatures."

It is one of the most untrue but widely held beliefs about us. I blame the library shelves stacked with magazines and best-selling books with simple tips on how to please a man as if every woman is a cooking class, opened legs, and bitten tongue away from having any man she wants. Even if that were true, it does no woman any good to have a man she wants if he doesn't show that he wants her, too, and more importantly, values her.

Most men initially identify the woman they want by the woman they believe they should want resulting in the pursuit of a "good" woman. The woman who's a good influence on him, a good look for him, honest, intelligent, and everything else we typically would characterize as "wife material."

Then, when he has her, realizes that he's still not satisfied because there's a yearning for something else than what she has to offer. It doesn't necessarily have to be better, but when he comes across those things in another woman, it's able to get his attention and make him risk everything he has in the "good woman" he worked so hard to get.

In fact, that woman is often far inferior by the standards he judged the first "good woman" by, and after everything hits the fan, even he can't explain why he made the decision to risk it. And while the responsibility to understand his actions are on him, as mothers and fathers who are raising young men, friends who will be asked to give counsel to our male friends, or even those of us with platforms that reach millions, we do the conversation around men a disservice by oversimplifying them by inadvertently oversimplifying the things a woman will task herself with bringing to a relationship for a man to appreciate.

When this happens, you create a generation of women that are changing themselves into whatever a man suggests since the simple things they were told to do don't produce the satisfaction they expected instead of focusing on becoming the best version of themselves with the confidence the right man will both want and value it. One problem is a man's suggestions may come from his current state as opposed to her best interests that he's supposed to have at heart.

So, a broken man will pressure her to fix him because a fixer is what serves his current state. He'll look for her to be the one to take his unresolved issues out on and put the responsibility on her to figure out how to make him whole again.

An immature man will tell her how she can double as his mother because that's what serves him. He'll want to be told to do the little things over and over again and to be coddled instead of required to grow up.

A lazy man will explain how she can be a better enabler. Instead of her being allowed the frustration of having to carry the financial and household responsibilities alone, he'll convince her she needs to stress herself out even more as she accepts the dwindling contribution he provides.

Players will guilt trip her if she dares to question the lies she knows he's feeding her. Sooner or later he'll have changed her into the most naïve version of herself until she's his doormat, so he can continue walking all over her into the bedrooms of other women, and she accepts it.

A man who's an opportunist will position her as his sponsor by leveraging her desperation if he senses any hint she doesn't want to be cast back into the relationship status she fears most, singleness.

But, the right man will focus more on ways they can both adapt to each other to achieve mutual relationship goals set forth from the beginning. That's the difference between him and those men who came before him who only looked to lower her relationship standards and force one-sided changes that the woman was to make to better suit his needs.

So, as a hard-working man, he'll require that she support him but also look for her to hold him accountable for supporting her as well, which serves their mutual goal of being each other's support system. As an honest man, he'll not only require transparency, but have nothing to hide either so they can build the foundation of trust that was the intention from the beginning. All of these things serve both of their needs, not just one person's preference.

So, how can a woman best position herself for the right one so she doesn't get caught up with the rest? Firstly, she must stop thinking strictly about what a man wants and start deciding whether he's even worth being wanted.

For many, that primary metric would be based on his relationship goals, or if he was marriage-minded, but these days, "marriage-minded" could describe a man who's looking for anything from a life-long partner to a life-long doormat.

This is not a knock on marriage because it is and always will be a beautiful thing, when done right. But if we've learned anything from the increasing divorce rate, it's that labels don't always define the contents. Not to mention the should-be divorce rate from marriages people are forcing themselves to allow to drag on, or the fact that Ike Turner had a wife, and so did Tiger Woods. This proves that even though a man who's found a wife has found a good thing, that wife could've just gotten found by the worst thing to ever happen to her, or vice versa.

So, finding or being found by a marriage-minded man isn't the problem, nor should it be a woman's number-one priority when it comes to deciding who she'll grow old with. Knowing how that man defines marriage, if he's found himself, and if it's the correct time in both of their lives to have found each other should be at the top of that list.

CHAPTER 18

❖

The New "Failed Relationship"

A wise man once said, "There's a thin line between love and hate." Well, through hundreds of conversations of drilling down to the root of toxic situations that started as a snowflake and ended up as an avalanche, I realized there's also a thin line between weathering a storm and weathering stupid.

"Why did he go and have a side baby on me…for the fifth time?" "I've caught him having sex with three different women this year alone. Does he really love me?" "We've been together four years and I just found out he's been married the entire time. What should I do?"

I literally cringed when I got these questions, and yes, each of those are actual inbox messages I've received. I know from the outside looking in, we can all see the clear answer, or at least what would be the obvious solution. But from the inside, I partly empathize with women in any of those situations, because it's not 100 percent their fault. I mean, it is, but if we're being really analytical, some of the blame should be divided between 1) how stupid love makes us all and 2) our aversion to letting a relationship "fail".

In a generation of "fall back games", hookups, and access to more options than ever before via social media and online dating, I can appreciate a fight for commitment as much as the next person. These days it's popular to throw in the towel before it even touches our sweat from trying to resolve whatever conflict showed up, but on the opposite end of that spectrum is a group of people who don't know where to draw the line between worth it and worthless. As a testament to our loyalty to a person, we'll kick a dead horse until our foot falls off and then wonder why it's so hard to walk away.

The reason is because after we go too far beyond the threshold of a relationship having a chance to not only last, but return to full health, we began to lose our own. We get away from the standards we had coming in and the confidence we deserve better begins to decay, so our decision making doesn't come from a place of what we will and will not tolerate, but rather what we're desperate to try and make happen because we don't know what we'll do if it doesn't.

So, at what point should we just let it go?

The answer: when you look at what you're tolerating and see that you'd be ashamed to tell the version of yourself you were before you got into the relationship. When you look at the issue, and you're no longer operating on evidence that it'll improve based on both you and your partner's effort, but mere hope because that's what you want. When you notice that you're the only one fighting for things to get back on track or realize that there's been nothing different about the most recent infraction that separates it from the others you've forgiven besides the date and excuses you were given as to why it happened. At that point, it's time to let it go, even if it's not for good.

This is not to be confused with a relationship break. Relationship breaks are more like intermittent singleness. The relationship is a mere exhale so that you can take a break from being single long enough to have your cake waiting for you after you're done eating it, too. Wanting out of the relationship temporarily is usually just a way to get a hookup-hall-pass and never actually fixes the issue. It just creates more that will return with the relationship breakers when they come back together.

But as for leaving the relationship altogether, there is no guarantee, implied or otherwise, of another chance. With this, you're requiring that the relationship as it is, and the person across from you in their current state is no longer good for you. Therefore, it must be completely done away with as far as your life goes, and there's not even a mention of trying again later because the intention isn't to eventually come back, it's to be done. Even if one person feels the other will come back or that they can go back if they wanted, that's not the agreement or conversation. No check-ins when the other person feels like they're starting to move on with another. No answers owed when you get interrogated about moving on to another.

It is actually over.

The significance of it isn't just in the technicality but so that if two people come back together, there's no relationship to thaw out that was waiting on ice. It must reconstruct from the ground up, and one or both people have to be brand new in their problem areas instead of just, "I decided I'm ready to come back."

This removes the disposability factor of the relationship that has many of us leaving when the temperature gets too hot, so we can cool off under the sheets with someone else.

But when we leave for good, regardless of what the future may bring, we're able to strictly focus on the self-love we need to heal and accept whatever feels right going forward with no prior commitment tying us to what may not belong in our next season. There's no guilt or accountability for the past because we only owe our future. However, I've seen many people get to this point, and either by their own definition or the assertion of others, consider their last relationship a "failure" because they're no longer in it.

There's no failure in leaving something and doing better because you left. There may have been a failure in your ability to have foreseen the outcome, but if you leave one place to go to another that's much better, that's not a failure, that was a pit stop.

Getting fired from a fast food job because your side business suddenly took off isn't a failure. Metaphorically, the fast food job would be your relationship while your side business would be the version of yourself you were growing into. When you increased, so did your standards that the current relationship you were in couldn't meet. It left you with two choices: either quit or get fired, in which either one would result in an upgrade of

Don't Forget Your Crown

freedom from what would otherwise have blocked the blessings of your future.

Sometimes we can't understand the value of an investment until we receive the return. What's your return on the investment of a hurtful, painful relationship? As cliché as it sounds, the lessons, but only if you take those lessons and apply them. The lessons, by themselves, mean nothing if you take them and repeat the same steps that landed you in the previous mess.

If you saw red flags that led to the deal breakers but entertained those same red flags because these came with a nicer smile, then no, you didn't get a positive return. If you gave your everything prematurely before and then required nothing additional before giving your all again, you didn't get your money's worth. Knowledge isn't power until it's acted on, and lessons don't profit you until you adjust for the better afterwards.

More importantly, loving the wrong person gives you additional tools to love the right one. It gives you the conviction when you're not doing what you're supposed to be doing to get it right because you know what it's like to be on the other side of the fence. It also makes giving your love to the right one more enjoyable and removes all doubt that you've found the one deserving of it. Showing that appreciation won't be something your partner longs for either, which will yield more motivation on his end to do more for you.

Last but not least, you benefit from the additional endurance. Although it wasn't best spent on prior relationships, the ability to persevere strengthened through the coping mechanisms you implemented in the wrong situation and the amount of time it's going to take to discourage you enough to leave. It's just important to remember that this muscle can be used for good or to your detriment but combined with learned lessons will only help you flourish.

Unless you are solely at fault for why the relationship went south, as in you violated the agreement, not just blamed yourself for it, then your past relationships were necessary stepping stones, training facilities, and bumpy roads headed towards your destination. They were not failures in reaching that destination.

Real failed relationships are the ones that are still intact from the outside looking in but broken beyond repair on the inside. They are the relationships where two people are pretending they're happy when behind closed doors. One of them may be, but the other is miserable, hopeless, and refuses to walk away from their own heartache. If a relationship is simply on the rocks, that's one thing, but when dysfunction becomes a fundamental piece of the union, it has failed, even if they're still together.

This is another way the phrase, "failed relationship" fails us all. It positions those who are single as the flunkies, while those in relationships are, by default, winners, which could cause undue envy and restlessness for those who don't know what's really going on when the "it" couple isn't posing for an Instagram ussie.

There are more relationships than we'd like to admit that consist of a man who allows verbal abuse to go unchecked because he doesn't want to have to pay out during a divorce, or a woman who accepts her man cheating so long as he comes home every night. But, those relationships are applauded the longer the two people in them suffer at the hands of each other therefore incentivizing prolonged dysfunction between them, while everyone else is taking their singleness for granted because they believe the grass is greener on the other side. And when you're constantly focused on grass that you think is greener, you neglect your own and end up with pesky weeds that you must deal with when you finally have company to join you on your lawn.

If we were to assess the success of a relationship not by its mere existence or by how long it's existed, but rather by its health, everything would change. Single people would shift the focus from simply getting into a relationship to preparing for a healthy one based on what they've learned from their previous ones. Couples would understand that suffering happens, but should only be tolerated when you're suffering on your way out of a situation, not suffering as a way of life. People who aren't meant for each other would stop wasting each other's time on the strength of how much time they've already wasted as if history with someone is the sole qualification for their presence in the future. People who pretend to be happy in their relationship would no longer be able to taunt others with fake relationship goals while going home to a partner who can't stand the sight of them. And people who are healing from a broken heart could stop feeling like a failure when really it was their partner who failed to see what they could've had if they'd been smart enough to match their effort.

CHAPTER 19

❖

Broken People Break People

I believe being raised in a single parent household is why I've always looked forward to being a father. Sure, there's the fear of bombing when you're doing something you've never witnessed firsthand, but then there's the advantage of having the things you missed so dearly stained on your heart so when it's time to provide them for your child, you'll know exactly what's needed, like heart-to-heart talks, confidence building, and protection.

So, long before I became a father, the thought of how I couldn't wait to have all of these with my children made me so anxious that I practiced doing the same things as an uncle. One of my dad rehearsals with my niece left me shook because while I'd done my share of forewarning about what to expect from little boys who liked her and how she should respond, I'd neglected one of the most important lessons that many adults still have yet to learn.

We were driving to the mall, and her playlist of hood-love songs was blasting through my truck. Of course, it was way inappropriate for her age, but if she can't listen to the music she normally listens to around me, then I doubt she'd ever feel comfortable expressing thoughts she normally has to me, so I gave her a pass. But I noticed through the song she was playing how the rapper was addressing some girl he claimed to love, saying things like "My life is so hard, and I've been through so much, and that's why I need you," and blah blah blah. It's not the first time I've heard it, but with my niece beside me, my radar caught what it'd missed the times before.

This is exactly the same thing broken men do to attract healers so they can break them. They speak to their pain, struggle, and hardship before going on about how its affected them. That's their segue to how a woman's value is priceless in their life. On the surface, it's endearing, but beneath those layers are forewarnings that she'll not only be the one he shows his damage to but also the one he damages.

I've heard, "You can't fix no man" a million times, but most times people think of a man who's lazy that they shouldn't waste time trying to motivate, or a cheater they shouldn't trouble themselves in trying to convince to settle down. Rarely do we address the connection women make to a man's pain and how a man can paint her as the cure he needs and won't have without her.

While I was listening to the song my niece played, even I found myself empathizing with the skillful portrayal of the man who lost loved ones, got betrayed by close friends, and deserted by his lovers when he was at his lowest moments in life. But, I was listening to music, not evaluating a love interest, and women who don't make the separation between the two end up paying for it later on down the line.

When a woman's heart opens to a man like that, she doesn't get to press pause when it hits home, his hurtful actions play on repeat with every time he apologizes and blames his brokenness on what he told her in the beginning. Starting out as friends, she did what friends do and listened to him tell her about these things while offering a listening ear but allowed things to go to the next level because of the good heart she thought she saw in him that turned her listening ear into a blind eye.

Maybe he does have a good heart, but a good heart counts for nothing inside a broken vessel. When a man is expressing how much he's been through and how he's looking for that one person that won't hurt him so he can finally heal, do not be that person. Why? Because before he heals, if he ever does, he will hurt whoever's close to him.

When it happens, the one he hurts will be so in love, she can't bring herself to see him for who he truly is. Even if friends and family are trying to bring her to her senses because they recognize that he's an abuser, she'll only see a wounded animal that's lashing out at her because she hasn't done enough to show him that she's not there to hurt him. That's how the cycle continues.

CHAPTER 20

❖

Can Men and Women Be Just Friends?

At the time Da'Naia and I had gotten reacquainted, I wasn't wilding out, living it up as bachelor of the year, but I was still in need of some rearrangements if she was going to have a permanent home in my life. I remember making the calls and texts to friend girls, letting them know in the nicest way possible that I didn't want to hear from them anymore. Not literally, but basically, relevant to how much access they had to me prior to my conversation with Da'Naia.

What's interesting is that I was never one to believe that men and women can't be friends. I'd heard old folks say that, but it didn't make sense because there's nothing that biologically dictates this. We decide what roles people are to play in our lives, nothing is predetermined. For instance, you (hopefully) don't date your siblings or your parents, not because you literally can't, but because you've (hopefully) decided that it would be disgusting. I've felt like having friends of the opposite sex would be the same if it weren't for our conditioning, or if we were to shed that misogynistic skin that a woman's value to us as men can only be sexual.

And as I got older, I found women that I thought were physically attractive, but that wasn't the value that attracted me to them. I was inspired by their drive, their creativity, strength, or what they stood for. Issa Rae, for example, is one of my biggest inspirations with her journey from YouTube to mainstream television. Although she's totally screwable by most men's standards and around the same age as me, I would feel lucky just for the opportunity to be her mentee or a part of her personal network. My admiration for her as a human far exceeds any attraction to her as a sexy woman to the point that even if she wanted to screw me, I wouldn't. A twenty-year-old me would jump at the chance, but as I've grown to understand women, I've grown to appreciate them as well beyond the fun we could have in the bedroom.

But when it was time to rebuild the foundation with the woman I loved, I pretty much cleaned house. Why? Because although I do believe men and women can be just friends, I don't believe there's room for more than one non-platonic foundation if you plan on any of them being a sturdy and life-long home. There was no need to lie to myself about it. Outside of a handful, I'd pretty much imagined or seen all of my friend-girls naked, and that was enough evidence that they needed to be repositioned either out of my life completely or at such a distance where our "friendship" downgraded to acquaintanceship at best, meaning we stayed connected on social media, maybe, but never blurred any lines of flirtation.

I've talked about this before, and it's always met with strong disagreements because "If he's an old friend that was before my new boyfriend, then the old friend stays." But the potential of a friendship is not about its age, it's about its beginnings. If it's an old flame, it needs to be put out or will eventually burn down the new house you're trying to build.

When you remain friends with someone you've had intimate experiences or feelings with, it's not guaranteed that something sexual will happen, but there's always a chance in which familiarity will only increase. And during a relationship, times of vulnerability provide those chances. Long-distance stints away from each other. Big arguments. Having your feelings hurt. Suspicions of cheating. And in case you have not noticed, we're all capable of doing things we wouldn't do under normal circumstances. But those things are almost always triggered by what our infrastructure is and what options are most accessible.

That's why people drink until they're sloppy drunk during times of extreme sadness who normally wouldn't touch alcohol. That's why others go to clubs they normally wouldn't be caught dead in when they're bored out of their minds. That's why people go back to exes they know very well haven't changed when they're so lonely they can't stand it. The thing we shouldn't do but are capable of shouldn't be anywhere close to us if we want to keep a perfect record of not indulging in it because as humans, we tend to measure our self-control by how we feel when we're not at our lowest point, and while no sin is greater than the other, that rule doesn't apply to relationship transgressions. There are some that weigh exponentially more than others, and one "slip up" with an old friend that you told your partner they didn't have to worry about is one of them.

If you don't use the right tone when talking to your partner, that can be forgiven. If you promise to be home by 10 p.m. in time to go to dinner, but show up at 11, there are ways to make up for that. But if you insert doubt in their mind that they're who you want and their heart is safe with you, it may take years to rectify that, if at all, and no "just a friend" was worth that risk to me.

That's not to say that I didn't form quality friendships afterwards with women, because I have, but the foundations were appropriate, and so is my investment in those friendships. The tone has been set in terms of the type of attention they receive from me, conversations we have, and amount of access they have to me. It's not all about pre-exterminating possibilities of cheating either. But the way we handle our friendships non-verbally communicates the priority of the romantic relationship we are in.

I probably could've pushed the envelope in some areas, being that Da'Naia was never the type to micro-manage me. Her mindset was that if she has to do that, then there's no point in even being in the relationship, and I agree. But I chose to restructure all my friendships in a way that was conducive for a happy home because that above all was my priority. That meant even my homeboys and I hung out differently.

Unless it was a special occasion, sure, I could go get a drink or two. But I had no business nightclub hopping or accompanying them to be the wingman anymore. Sure, it's a bit of a buzz-kill, but I didn't want the buzz more than I wanted to build a future with my woman so anything that could compromise that wasn't of interest to me anymore.

The way I handled social media changed as well. I like sex and sexy things just as much as the next man. Well, maybe not as much as some pervs out there, but I'm no nun. However, I'm no dummy either, and I knew I couldn't play dumb when it came to my conduct on social media needing some tweaks, which I've yet to see become a relationship standard in our generation.

Most guys I know feel like it's acceptable to like the same pics they did before or scroll through the same accounts they did before they got into a relationship, so long as they don't "actually cheat." And with many women's paranoia of being seen as "crazy" for wanting their man to respect them and their relationship, the passes they give aren't helping. But if we're considering non-verbal communication a real thing, then social media conduct needs to be accounted for.

I'm sure at some point in medieval times, winking or licking your lips at someone was seen as harmless. But today, if someone does that to you, they've all but put their tongue down your throat. Some of us remember when "poking" on Facebook was a strange thing because we didn't quite know what it meant, but now if someone does it that you're not already familiar with, it's downright creepy.

The point that I'm making is that some of these actions and their meanings evolve with time, so our behavior in an effort to respect our relationship should as well. Yes, in the mid 2000s, "liking" someone's picture was innocent. But today, we know that depending on the type of picture, how many pictures we're liking, and how long ago the picture was posted, our "liking" a picture could mean anything from "Congrats, I'm proud of you," to "I want you on top of me, now."

Disregarding what this could mean or what signals it could send is disregarding what end result could come of it, which is easy to do until you can't undo the damage that you've done. While every person's comfort level with their partner's behavior is different, the rule of thumb should be that as a man, if you wouldn't compliment another woman in person in front of your woman with the same attire and pose she's showing in the picture, then you shouldn't "like" it online either.

Sure, if a girl just had a child, is graduating from college, or just started her new job, nothing's wrong with liking that picture. But if she's showing camel toes, nipple rings, twerking, sitting on a bathroom sink, or anything sexually suggestive, we know good and well our "like" on that picture isn't rooted in pure thoughts.

The same goes for women, too. If a guy is free-balling in his sweat pants with a semi-erection for a 3-D effect, then there's no reason a happily taken woman should be expressing admiration because just like other behavior while in a relationship, you are a reflection of your partner, or rather the respect you have for your partner. And putting your attraction on the radar of someone outside of your relationship may not be cheating, but it's sugar-coated disrespect towards your relationship that will eventually cause the same damage as if you'd just cheated in the first place.

This is the point where people play dumb and start talking about "visual creatures" or "insecurities", but it has nothing to do with that. Men are visual creatures, yet that doesn't absolve us from our responsibility to be respectful creatures as well, because if a woman did many of the things we try to normalize as "a man being a man" then we'd be some jealous creatures, too. The same goes for our insecurities, and we all have some, but insecurities don't excuse disrespect when it's the disrespect that causes the insecurities.

Is it only men who blur these lines? No. But sugar-coated disrespect for men is what casual disrespect is for women. The difference is that instead of passing off this behavior as something we do because we're being "nice" or as a better alternative to cheating, casual disrespect is something many women don't' notice at all, and when brought to their attention either feel like it's justified or should be tolerated because that's who they are.

So instead of blatantly degrading a man by calling him names, it comes in the form of snarks, rolling eyes during conversation, walking off on him in mid-sentence when he's genuinely upset and trying to explain something, looking at something else to communicate she doesn't care what he's saying to her, etc.

All of these and other body language that says he's not important and neither are his feelings or thoughts about her behavior are casual disrespect and will ruin a relationship as effectively as anything else, even if it doesn't end the relationship. These actions often get blamed on what the man is saying or something he did, but communication should never regress to shots fired, whether directly or subtly, and if what he's doing is that bad, there's a way to let him know that, respectfully.

If he's not deserving of that respect, or if he disregards your attempt to be civil as you present your perspective then he's not exhibiting behavior that'll sustain a healthy relationship and your only option is to either leave or remain with a man who'll eventually bring out the worst in you.

The moral of the story is, you must be all in or all out. With all the things set up to make your relationship fail these days, two people who honestly want one to work shouldn't put any additional obstacles in their way, and there's no bigger obstacle than ones that covertly compromise the integrity of the relationship.

Old flames that can smolder from the shadows of the friend circle, same-sex friends who aren't made to respect new relationship goals, social media behavior that doesn't align with those goals, and casual disrespect that breeds resentment more than effectively communicated points are all ways to self-sabotage a relationship. While it's easy to frame insecurities, social media, or sensitivity for the downfall, the real culprit, disregard, will continue to wreak havoc on your relationships until you face it head-on.

CHAPTER 21

❖

Men Don't Know How to Express Feelings

As a young man, I remember feeling like my emotions were germs. Being sad, frustrated, hurt, or even borderline depressed was never given a place to exist without being either scrutinized by peers or just looked over as something I'd eventually get over by authoritative figures.

If a girl was caught crying, she was immediately tended to and somebody probably needed to apologize, but for me and other boys, it was something we could never get caught doing without being punished with either ridicule or apathy because it was viewed as weak.

I turned to writing, poetry to be specific, as an outlet for my emotions. My notebook never judged me, and there was nothing I could do to erase the emotions I had, so writing about them made me feel like they were being managed. I was able to spend a lot of time with myself in my developmental years through that, and it's partly what I credit for mitigating what could've been the damage done by not having my father. But, unfortunately, not every boy finds a healthy way to deal with his softer side, which results in years of suppressed pain or toxic ways of acting out any time those emotions arise.

So, the general conception that men have a hard time expressing their feelings is rooted in truth, but in today's relationships has opened the door for more disingenuous copouts than emotionally developmental solutions.

Yes, it is difficult for many men to open up about vulnerabilities without feeling like less of a man, but our general feelings as it relates to women are pretty clearly expressed. If we like a woman, we show it. If we're only sexually attracted to a woman, have no respect for her, are intimidated by her, or believe we want to marry her, we make those things obvious.

But, if a woman is not careful, she'll let her high hopes, denial, emotional defense mechanisms, or his explanations distort the messages being relayed about how he feels about her.

I've seen thousands of women looking for the secret code to things their man was doing when he wasn't being secretive to begin with. For instance, one woman asked me what it meant when a man told her she wasn't allowed to have male friends without his approval and needed to check in with him before she spent time with her friend girls and family as well. While the clear message here was that he felt like she was an object to be controlled, not someone he saw as his equal, the communication was lost due to his explanation that it was his job to protect her, and as his woman, she needed to do her part to allow him the ability to.

It's almost like going to a dealership and purchasing a new Mercedes, except the only thing "Mercedes" about it is the logo glued to the back of the junkyard clunker. No matter how badly you wanted a car, your good sense should tell you that you have no business paying for one thing and getting another, so you'd be better off just walking until you can get your money's worth. However, there are women who apparently believe otherwise, because so long as the logo on the back looks good, they're driving whatever they get handed keys to and paying top dollar in terms of the value they have to offer.

Want to know what else is a clunker with a luxury vehicle logo on it? Getting told the divorce is almost final, but the "bitter wife" won't sign the papers or is intentionally drawing things out despite him being done. More than likely, she's drawing it out because he hasn't given her any other thoughts on his intentions for the marriage since he told her, "I do."

Getting told that he's taking his child's mother out for her birthday with the kids, or sleeping over there on the holidays for the kids when it's not just for the kids, it's for the family they still have together is a commonly sold junkyard special.

But one of the most run-down vehicles advertised as top of the line is the one where you two just met but he's too busy working to ever spend real quality time with you or even have a few conversations on the phone. Truth is, it's likely he may have to work one or two days more than expected, which could spill in time you two had set aside beforehand, but if you're someone he's excited about getting to know, he'll reschedule the time you two missed much sooner than later. At worst, he'll pick up the phone and spend an hour or so connecting with you through conversation, but nobody is so busy for two or three consecutive months, they have no room for what they truly want to do.

This means that a man having some difficulties expressing his feelings shouldn't stop you from protecting yours from what it is he may be saying to you with his behavior. Unless he's mute, he's going to be talking, but the question comes down to what it is you're listening to, or better yet, what are you ignoring? If you find yourself misreading the men you date regularly, then your answer to that question may be "your intuition."

The term gets thrown around quite often, so for clarity, I define a woman's intuition as that voice in the back of your head that you hear when something doesn't add up but impulsively shrug off because you confuse it as overthinking, trust issues, or just no big deal. But what separates that voice from the rest of the thoughts floating around your mind is how distinct it is when things all hit the fan that you were right from the beginning.

That's your intuition, and through knowing yourself, you'll learn to tell its voice apart from the beginning, before you learn the hard way.

No matter who or what you believe in, you must admit that men and women were designed differently beyond our genitals. Men tend to be more muscular, that's our advantage for survival. Women were given intuition as their advantage for survival. We were created to work together as a team so these two things would balance out, but in relationships, we unfortunately have gotten to a point where we use these against each other. That's why men use fear of physical harm as a form of control, but if the battle is a matter of mind games, women almost always have the upper hand. Women only lose mind games when they're not aware they're being played, but when they decide to, men are huge underdogs.

Both of these are sad situations and nobody should be aiming to resort to them, but the power of a woman's intuition can be used just as effectively in battle, as it can be used to avoid battle altogether. Unfortunately, with men making the rules of relationships and well-intended yet ill advice being passed down from older generations, that weapon which would serve more as a shield before a woman has established who her partner will be, gets ignored from fear of being "crazy" or ruining what could've been a good thing.

When used properly, intuition is somewhat of a translator of reality, if a woman is emotionally healthy. If she's still heartbroken, it'll get drowned out by paranoia. If a woman hasn't healed from having her trust in men broken, it'll get drowned out by those trust issues. But if she's taken the time she needs from her last relationship, she's reclaimed her crown, and she's spent enough time around a man to have gotten a pretty good idea of who he is, then her intuition, if she uses it, will bring the truth out of hiding one way or the other.

It'll tell her when his actions aren't aligned with his words. It'll tell her when he's acting strange, or a little more nervous than usual. It'll tell her when he's distant or starting baseless arguments just to have a reason to leave the house. It'll start moving her to places she normally wouldn't go, without consciously understanding why, just to show her something she needed to see at that exact moment. That's why so many women "forget things" at home and have to turn back around to go to the house, or just felt like coming home from their girls' trip early to find him in bed with another woman (or man). When a woman says, "Something told me to..." that's her intuition.

In a healthy relationship, that intuition is what she uses to sniff out fake friends or give him extra special attention that night because she could sense that he was more stressed than usual from work. Her intuition works for his benefit when he's acting in her best interest, but when that changes, its role does as well.

Two things will try to stop it, one of them being love.

Unfortunately, love makes us dumb. It's the risk we all take when we fall into it, but the good thing is, its effect on our intelligence isn't permanent. We don't remain dumb forever, and if whatever actions triggered the shift in the woman's intuition persists, it'll eventually bring her to her senses unless the second effort to stop it is in full effect: manipulation. If his manipulation about how this is all in her head and she's "crazy" for even entertaining the idea that something doesn't feel right is planted in fertile soil of naivety or brokenness, it can take such strong root where even her intuition can't save her.

That's what makes the conversation around manipulation so important to have, and equally important, the stress of how valuable a woman's intuition is. Some people think it's just a hocus-pocus made-up thing, but it's as real as the scientifically higher testosterone levels in boys.

I've heard false equivalencies of our gut feeling to a woman's intuition before, which is as comparable as a paper plane to a fighter jet. The aim may be the same, but the ability couldn't be more set apart.

So, in a relationship, if a woman is feeling like her man is not telling her something, there's no need to dismiss it as simply a man who doesn't know how to express his feelings. Could it be? Sure. But the intuition should let her know. If he's legitimately having a hard time being vulnerable with her or explaining himself in a way that doesn't make him feel like less of a man, a woman should remind him that she won't judge him for whatever comes out and encourage him to take the step forward in his evolution as a communicator. She should be patient with him, no interruption, no discouraging non-verbal cues, and allow him to make progress in that area. If he's really committed, he'll force himself to make this progress since communication is the cornerstone of relationships.

However, if his "can't express his feelings" seems like more of a copout to hide something, a woman only has one job to do: trust the intuition.

CHAPTER 22

❖

Is it Unnatural to be Monogamous?

The conversation about how men have a hard time expressing our feelings came up more with my male acquaintances and followers than it did with women. That's usually how conversations go with men, we don't scratch our heads trying to figure women out nearly as much as we scratch our heads trying to figure ourselves out. That could be because we've given up on figuring women out because they're "too complicated", or because we believe figuring them out is unnecessary since there is always a woman who will bend to whatever shape we like, or because we've been lied to about our role in this world.

I personally believe it's a bit of all three, but that's not the point. During a conversation with a new friend of mine I met at the gym--we'll call him Earl--I was presented with the theory that men are bad at relationships because we're trying to be monogamous when that's not what we were designed to be. Earl was older than me by about 20 years, so he talked to me like he was schooling his son on life when he told me this. He said that since polygamy dated back into ancient Egyptian times and there were so many more women than men, that meant there's supposed to be multiple women for every man as well.

To be honest, I never gave polygamy much thought, and at the time didn't know just how prevalent this belief was among men, and even some women. Having multiple women on a serious level seemed unfair, and I could never see a man, myself included, okay with being serious with a woman that gave herself to multiple men.

However, there is a growing number of people who believe giving their all to a person who shares themselves among many should be the way of life. And it is, but a really sad one.

Yes, polygamy dates back to ancient times. Egypt, Greece, and all the other places where slavery was also practiced, and just like slavery, being an ancient (even though slavery isn't that ancient) practice doesn't make something right. In fact, in most cases, it means it's the exact opposite and predates new information and advancements we've acquired since.

As for our biological makeup, I'm well-aware of the endless sexual appetite we're capable of. This is what I feel like most men premise their passion behind the polygamist argument over, anyway. Do you really think men believe we "deserve" to have the emotional needs of a woman we're responsible for meeting multiplied? Do you think we want three or four times the children we're responsible for being full-time fathers for? Do you honestly believe that we want to increase the amount of hard conversations we already don't like having or amount of quality time we're asked to spend with one woman that we claim is hard to come by? Or does it make sense that we want to have access sexually to multiple women without having to hide or feel guilty because of it?

I get it, we have a big sexual appetite, but polygamy isn't the answer. Is our appetite natural? Sure. But we naturally love a lot of unhealthy food, full of fats and sugar. Does this mean we're biologically wired for heart disease? No. We're biologically wired to see where an over indulgence, especially on the wrong things, could lead to a negative end result and therefore have been wired with the ability to shape our behavior to avoid that if we value our health.

It's no different when it comes to our body's sexual urges. Packaging our desire for the freedom to indulge in different women in the appealing box of "natural" doesn't change that that lifestyle belongs in single life, not relationships. Don't just take it from me, take it from our creator.

Even without a relationship title, if we are spending relationship time, and partaking in relationship activities with a person, seeing them do the same thing with another person involuntarily causes pain, or if things had carried on long enough, heartbreak. That hurt we feel isn't a social construct, it's innate, which is evidence that whoever designed sex and other intimate engagement to be so enjoyable didn't create it to be shared with multiple people, at least not simultaneously.

Since heart disease is to undisciplined eating habits what heartbreak is to being simultaneously intimate with multiple people, then polygamy is no different than a daily buffet of doughnuts except the sister wives will be the ones who end up with clogged arteries while the polygamist husband stuffs his face.

So, wanting to have multiple long-term relationship partners makes sense, but only if we're going to admit that we honestly don't care about women, or at least the effect the relationship construct would have on them regardless of what they say to deny it. At best she'd be numb, but I can't see any woman honestly giving the best of herself to a man emotionally and physically and being 100 percent okay with seeing him give himself to another woman.

So, if we're hell-bent on the natural order of things, and we know our hearts were naturally made to function unbroken and without being made numb, then common sense minus ego equals the admittance that polygamy is bullshit.

With that said, my goal is not to dictate what decisions you make in your life nor judge you for them. If voluntarily being with someone who's not all for you is your desire, then you've hit the jackpot with polygamy. But if being with one person who's also exclusively for you is what you want, then your jackpot exists as well, and monogamy that's founded on more than just love is the pathway to it.

CHAPTER 23

Love Didn't Do It

S ome of the best conversations happen when you're just alone with your partner, cut off from the news, timelines, TV stations, and texts. Soft music doesn't hurt, but just enough to where it doesn't intrude on the space you're sharing physically and mentally. There's a connection that's hard to describe in those moments, but it's as distinct as it is necessary when you're looking to stay connected as a couple.

During one of these, what I called "vibe sessions" with my girl, I began seriously thinking about marriage. Of course, I'd thought of it before, but it had only been in the way you'd look at a diving board versus now standing with your foot on the first step of the ladder to go up and jump off.

We'd gotten to a good place together and showed no signs of being removed from that good place any time soon. We'd enjoyed great moments in our previous relationship, but this didn't feel like a moment. This felt like the status quo and had been so for over a year at that point. Our communication had matured tremendously on both sides and incorporating these times to just sit and think together allowed us to mentally remain joined at the hip.

I decided to use one of these opportunities to relieve myself of curiosity that'd been marinating on me since we first reconnected.

"Do you think we made a mistake?" I asked her. "When we first got together, back in school. Do you think that was a mistake?"

I asked because I wanted to know what she thought of our younger years. We'd not discussed it much as not to relive the past, but I wasn't trying to relive it, I just wanted to know.

She responded, "Well, if I could go back and do it again knowing what I know now, I wouldn't."

My heart sank, but I didn't show it on my face.

I responded, "So, are you saying it was a mistake?"

"Yes," she added. "But not us dating. I made the mistake of being so excited by your potential. I took my eye off your reality. That's the part I wouldn't do a second time around."

What she continued to explain completely changed the way I thought about potential. Whereas I knew I was an unfinished product upon meeting her, far underdeveloped compared to who I had grown into by the time we had this conversation, I also knew we all were potential on some level, including her. We all had room to grow and should all be allowed that room to grow without judgment.

Except, judgment is necessary for survival, and all room to grow isn't created equal. Think of a car that needs some repairs. There are repairs that can wait until your next paycheck, like say the stereo system going out or maybe the interior lights don't come on when you open the door. Sometimes people never fix those things and even forget they need fixing until someone else points it out.

Then there are cars with a tail light out, low tread on tires, or even squeaky brakes. Still, not an absolute emergency, but definitely something to tend to in the near future, and in the meantime, the car need only be used when necessary.

But then there are things like a transmission failure or engine being blown. Until these types of repairs are made, a car is pretty much useless. With good judgment, you can plan according to the repairs with minimal inconvenience to your schedule or if need be, just get another mode of transportation altogether.

In hindsight, she didn't quite see me as having my engine blown, but I was certainly the squeaky brake-level of a vehicle. I was of some use but should've been left in the garage until I got my repairs done because I couldn't handle the daily work of being her romantic partner, which eventually wore my squeaky brakes completely bare.

As to not come off defensive, I refrained from bringing up the thought that we should've both been parked for a few more years of repairs, but it did cross my mind. Relationships are serious business and we weren't ready. I was much further behind the eight-ball than she, but I don't think either of us had any idea of what we were getting ourselves into but getting into it made it crystal clear to me that what we were now into was something I wanted to remain in for the rest of my life.

I thought my decision to propose to her would be based on our love reaching its pinnacle like never before, but it wasn't. We had plenty love for each other and were as in love as any couple could be, but when I'd confirmed it was time to put a ring on her finger, it was from a place of understanding that we needed so much more than love to make a marriage work, and we finally had it.

I would even go so far as to say that love in a romantic context is overrated. Love doesn't keep your voice down going forward when your partner tells you that your tone makes them feel uncomfortable, respect does. Love doesn't tell your opposite-sex friend there are new boundaries they must adhere to now that you're in a relationship, consideration does. Love doesn't cook more despite cooking not being your strong suit, selflessness does. Love doesn't ignore advances from attractive people during long-distance stints within the relationship despite there being a good chance you wouldn't get caught, self-control does.

Love doesn't make time out of an already busy schedule to spend quality time together, priorities do. Love doesn't allow your partner space and time they need to have a life outside of you, trust does. Love doesn't map out physical, financial, and relationship goals to achieve together and a plan to ensure success, forethought does.

Most of us have been taught that love, or as the media calls it, "true love" is a full package with all those things within, but it's not. We were born with the ability to love, even as toddlers, but everything else had to be acquired over the years as we grew up. That's why despite loving our parents, it didn't stop us from being disrespectful, disobedient, and dishonest at times. We had to be taught at the hands of discipline and following our parents' example, and even then these things had to be practiced until they eventually became a part of our identity. The same concept applies to romantic relationships.

I had been disciplined by my own self-inflicted chaos, and while my relationship lived to tell the story, it wasn't the love that did it. No longer operating from a place of brokenness, naivety, selfishness, foolishness, and youth, and individually growing and healing as needed is what did it. Love was just a bonus, the way it was meant to be.

CHAPTER 24

❖

Why Buy the Cow If He Can Get the Milk for Free?

"First comes love, then comes marriage, then comes the baby in the baby carriage," is like singing, *Jingle Bells*. Riding in a one-horse open sleigh is a nice thought, and if you end up doing it, good for you. But many people have had a very Merry Christmas without doing so, and many people have also enjoyed happy homes without love, marriage, and a baby happening in that exact order.

If you can't tell by now, I'm not a very conventional thinker, and the same held true when it came to my wife and I's living situation. I understood very well what my mom and other elders of my family taught me I was "supposed" to do and shacking up wasn't one of them, but with rising living costs of rent for at least one of our apartments being left vacant on the regular to be with the other and sky-high gas prices to make those drives, I hated having two separate homes.

Of course, this is anyone's personal decision, and to this day, I don't see a right or wrong way to go about this, but when we found out she was carrying our first child, it was a no-brainer to ask her if she was okay moving in together. Her family was thousands of miles away, and I wanted full access to be there for whatever she needed without having to plan for a drive to get to her first. Marriage, as far as I was concerned, was inevitable so long as she said yes, so my sole priority shifted to preparing us for a child, and with her consent, that's what I did.

But in the process, there was a conversation that came up in one of my Instagram live chats that struck a chord when a woman asked me what I thought constituted as exclusive husband privileges. Before answering, I posed the question to everyone else on the chat, somewhere around two thousand or so people, and while the answers themselves didn't disturb me, the reasoning behind those answers did.

I saw comments stating, "sex," "cooking," "cleaning," and "lending him money," should be husband privileges. I was thinking along the lines of cosigning property and quitting a dream job to help him to pursue his career goals, things that I felt were better fit for a situation where "'till death do us part" was the expressed understanding, but sprinkled within their answers were phrases like, "Why buy the cow when he can get the milk for free?" That's where I stepped in, veering from the original question onto what I thought was a more fundamental area that needed to be addressed.

After prefacing my thoughts with the disclaimer that religious people may not like what I had to say, I continued with, "Any man who's buying the cow shouldn't be buying it for the milk. He should be buying the cow because he wants the cow."

For conversational purposes of not continuing to interchange-ably refer to a woman as a cow, let's just stop that now. But, when a woman is in a relationship, it is 100 percent her prerog-ative what things she's comfortable doing or not doing before being married and the same goes vice versa. But if a man is marrying a woman because he wants those "husband privileg-es" like sex and housekeeping, that woman is getting a raw deal.

Things that you do can be replaced, but the woman that you are cannot. If a man is marrying you for the things that you do, you are simply a filler. You are less of the one he wants, and more the one who's going to provide what he wants.

While I would say both wives and husbands need to contrib-ute to the marriage to their fullest potential, the commitment shouldn't be predicated on those things, and for the commit-ment not to be predicated on the things, neither should the motivation to have made the commitment. If you come down with an illness and can't cook, you shouldn't have to worry that your marriage is on the brink of falling apart. If you go through a depression or some other biological issue that prevents you two from having sex, you shouldn't have to lose sleep about him remaining committed.

However, if you present yourself as an honest, trustworthy woman but after marrying him he finds that you are a habitual liar and you can't be trusted any further than he can spit, then yes, it makes complete sense that he'll rethink his commitment since he's not getting the woman he fell in love with. If he pres-ents himself as kind and gentle and turns out to be a man who's cruel and heartless, there's no reason you should stay hitched either, because that's not the man you married.

So back to the original phrase, when you're looking to marry someone, you're not looking at them in terms of what they do, but in terms of what characteristics make them who they are and how that fits into who you are so you two can become one. The characteristics that make you who you are in the proportion they're within you as well as the experiences that shaped you, values, beliefs, and vision for your future come in one package, yours. Marriage or not, if he's with you for that, then no one else can offer an upgrade or replacement because he can only get it with you. However, if he marries you for milk, then he can go to any grocery store cooler and pick a jug, and commitment on any level won't even be a requirement.

Again, I understand the thinking behind the premise of not going too hard or doing too much for a man who's not committed to the highest degree, but this is another area we need to evolve if we're going to set the stage for more lasting and healthy relationships. Playing into those men who are motivated to marry because they're trying to get a woman's milk is to also play into the treating a relationship like a product to be consumed instead of a growing, living being to be cared for as long as it lives.

Ask yourself, "If I'm charging him the price of marriage in exchange for my milk, what happens after the transaction has cleared?"

That brings us back to the point I made earlier about a man being a prize to continuously earn his prize over the course of the relationship. If you get a man with that mindset, you'll avoid the commonly settled for man who is either complacent once he gets his milk for "free", or pays up in the form of matrimony, and sits back afterwards with a receipt to point to should you ever complain about feeling a little milked out.

Does that mean you should go handing your milk out all over town? No. What you should do is, first, focus less on having a man marrying you, and focus more on what the man is pledging his commitment to, which should be two things. One, you, the person, and two, the health of the relationship you require.

The things you do in the relationship should be a byproduct of who you are, and a bonus to your package, but not the sole or even primary focus of his. If you choose to wait to do them until after you're married, that's fine. But if you do them before you're married, you can always pull the plug if you feel like they're not being appreciated or deserved per his reciprocity. I'm one of those people that believe in putting your best foot forward in a relationship, and sometimes that best foot forward needs to ease off the gas a bit if the steering wheel is turning in the wrong direction.

Translation: If you feel like the things you're doing to make him comfortable and happy in the relationship are incentivizing complacency, stop. If you feel like they're reinforcing laziness on his part, stop. While no one should expect a relationship to be a direct split of 50/50 contribution all the time, if anyone begins to feel unsure about the future of the relationship due to the other's actions, then it's fair for that person who's unsure to focus their attention on the problem area until it's been addressed, which may result in pulling back from the pouring on of those relationship perks, a.k.a. husband privileges.

But, so long as he keeps the priorities in their proper place, the relationship will move forward as healthy ones do instead of coming to a stand-still before matrimony or even worse, afterwards, like dying relationships do. The extracurricular enjoyments can serve as luxuries of this healthy relationship instead of being mandated expectations while progression towards the goals set forth in the beginning get put on the backburner.

CHAPTER 25

Marriage is Everything BUT Settling Down

Since then, my entire life has changed. First, my daughter was born. Healthy, pale, and looking just like me. I cried, of course, but the moment I held her in my hands, I felt like everything I'd been working so hard for professionally and personally had come full circle.

During my childhood, my siblings and I shared a room and bed, but my daughter would be able to have her own. I didn't have my father in the house or at all for that matter growing up, but my daughter would. The best part of all, she would be able to witness what a healthy, loving marriage looked like, firsthand, instead of only seeing them play out on TV.

We're in a day and age where marriage seems to be under attack. There's some "modern" version being promoted left and right from open marriages or what I call "swingerships" to people who think marriage is just a piece of paper.

There are practical purposes for marriage, especially if you're going to be building a life and family with someone where one person's going to take on the role of strictly supporting the other and mostly raising the children, but for me it's much deeper than that.

As a man, there's a sense of pride you get from being able to proclaim not just your love, but your commitment to the one you love in front of those who know you both best. The changing of your names to create a joint identity in the world that history will recognize when it's all said and done and placing reminders of that privilege to do so on your ring finger as a symbol of your commitment removes the "I" out of your decision making and replaces it with "we."

When there's no higher representation of your intentions for your future with someone, no further intertwined into their life that you can be, it creates such an intimate atmosphere in the relationship that bachelor life, even in its prime, can't come close to competing with.

Marriage has always been slandered as "settling down," especially for men, but it should be referred to as "leveling up." That's more appropriate for the effect it's had on my wife and I from our conversations, to the business decisions, to affection, and more, and when I talk to other married men, we seem to share that sentiment.

One thing I don't have in common with most married people is my level of discretion, particularly when it comes to social media. It's been a commonly asked question over the years as to why I'm especially discreet with my personal life when it's most popular for relationships to make their way boldly into the world of social media on every date, holiday, proposal, wedding, honeymoon, and more.

I don't believe anything to be wrong with that when done in moderation, but I've seen the effects of going overboard which seems to be happening more and more these days. There comes a lack of connection on dates because going out becomes more about showing the moment to online friends as opposed to enjoying the moment with your partner, as well as an over-investment into what people are saying about that moment. Add to that the time it takes to keep up with what's being said, and you can see how each of these things help destroy relationships that may have otherwise survived the turbulence all relationships go through.

For instance, couples go through shit. It's a part of life and always has been. What hasn't always been a part of life are platforms where a crowd of outsiders have been keeping up with your relationship through your personal documentation who now notice the tone of your posts indicate trouble in paradise. Just like any other plot twist, this evokes curiosity and therefore probing. During a vulnerable moment where you're overflowing with thoughts and are near desperately in need of someone to relate to how you feel, the temptation to oblige them could cause you to overshare what's going on in your relationship when it's really none of their business. Nevertheless, the moment you do, that energy will make its way into your relationship and could become a permanent consequence to a temporary emotion.

Because now your partner is humiliated, and so are you. It's no longer a matter of communicating better with each other but managing outside perceptions of others and even after a solution is implemented internally, agendas are composing externally and so is the chatter about what else is going on in your relationship. Whereas it may not have been much of a problem before, the dust still has yet to settle, and the feeling isn't quite the same in those selfies you post in which if you've really gotten in deep, this will hurt you and reinvite negative energy to pollute the connection with your partner all over again.

That's just one scenario I've seen play out, and likely the most common next to the on and off again every month couple that ruthlessly defames each other one day and then are back to relationship "goals" the next. While it is tacky, it's everyone's right to be tacky, however, that's not my style.

I subscribe to the higher end of privacy, and the few couples I've seen who do the same agree that the grass is much greener on this side. I once believed this was just a matter of preference since some people are introverts, but dare I say, privacy can result in a higher chance for longevity and quality of the relationship?

When anything goes wrong in life, a necessary step in the moving-on process is putting it behind you. If you lose your job, you get another and forget about the last. If you lose your wallet, you get another, replace everything inside, and forget about it. Any behavioral scientist will tell you that living in the past is one of the leading causes of depression as well as an ineffective and unhealthy way to deal with any painful experience.

In relationships, having breakdowns in trust, understanding, or connection on any level is bound to happen. The sex won't be great at some point. Somebody will be late picking the kids up from daycare or forget to ask what's wrong when the other is visibly bothered. A line will get blurred with somebody, or questions about a coworker's comments via text will arise. Something will happen that must be sorted out, and once it is, it needs to be left in the past.

The problem is, social media doesn't let you leave anything in the past. People's pics, tweets, etc. get dug up every day and resurfaced for them to answer to, and a relationship is no different. This won't guarantee the demise, but it attaches a leech to emotional wounds that result from things not going so well, making it difficult for you and your partner to bounce back. Without the round table discussion of your personal business, you get what has become the luxury of privacy to handle your issues in-house without having to waste energy on answering to outsiders about it.

In some situations, all hands must be on deck, but they can't be if you're trying to dissect the opinions' of others who have made themselves at home on the living room couch of you and your partner from their smart phone.

So, how much privacy is too much when it comes to social media? None. As mentioned before, if your man posts everything but you, that can certainly be a red flag, but healthy relationships have existed many centuries longer than Facebook and Instagram. They weren't a prerequisite then, and they aren't one now, but if your relationship is going to have a presence on these platforms, then rules for engagement should be established within the conversation on the relationship's membrane.

CHAPTER 26

Relationship Membrane

I distinctly remember sitting in my Biology 101 class during freshman year thinking how useless the info my professor passionately disseminated upon us would be in the real world, and I couldn't have been more wrong. Surprisingly, plant cells and relationships have quite a bit in common, one of them being membranes.

To save some of you a trip to Google, a membrane is a barrier that controls what comes in and what's allowed to go out of a cell. All relationships have them, or rather, they should.

Without one, things from the outside of the relationship are allowed to penetrate at will and immediately cause an explosion. Such-and-such said this, so one of you has an attitude or suspicion that turns into snooping and privacy being violated without any other indicator that what such-and-such said is founded in any truth. Or your mom doesn't like your partner so now the marriage is called off until mom changes her mind.

When the membrane is weak, the nucleus suffers, but if a membrane is unbalanced, as in one person believes in being uncompromisingly stubborn to anything the other person may have concerns about from outside the relationship, then the nucleus doesn't just suffer, it's the cause of the issue.

For instance, if you got some recommendations about locations to travel to and your man refuses to hear anything you have to say about traveling somewhere your friend recommended because he doesn't like her, that's an unbalanced membrane. If you've gotten a screenshot sent to your DM of your man supposedly texting another woman, and he shuts it down without hearing what you have to say, or if it's circulating among your friends that your man has been overly friendly with other women at the bars he frequents, yet your man won't entertain the conversation because they're just, "hating," that's an issue.

Or as a man, if you've gotten some helpful insight from someone about relationships, but even when you respectfully bring it up in general conversation, your woman shuts it down the moment she realizes this advice came from another woman, that's a nucleus problem. At that point, there's either something being hidden, or a complete disregard for the feelings of the person bringing the information to the forefront and has nothing to do with the outside anymore.

Strong membranes are meant to be selective barriers to the outside, not communication barriers within. There is no one way to properly set your membrane, but I'll share the one my wife and I use that has wiped out 100 percent of our arguments triggered by anything happening outside the four walls we live in.

1. There is a clear understanding of what information is privy to outsiders, including social media. Anything outside of relationship status and where we last vacationed to is pretty much off limits. Topics of any disagreements, sex, financial issues or rewards, and date nights are off limits. Any exception, including this list, is discussed beforehand but as a consistent of our marriage, we've found that this maintains a comfortable level of privacy for us both.

    Because of my social media presence, my platform is especially off limits to anything directly featuring her or our children. As an introvert, she's never cared much for the attention, and it's allowed her to maintain the normalcy she prefers over being recognized when out in public.

2. Any outside advice is fair to entertain but won't be accepted or acted on until it's been discussed and we both agree. Reinforcements of already determined rules don't count, but new information is fun to debate and oftentimes can add value. The latest outside advice we received was to consistently check each other's love tank as mentioned in the book, *The Five Love Languages*, which since we've been doing has kept us both on our toes in terms of pouring into each other without getting so bogged down with everyday life that we forget.

3. In times of pain or misunderstanding, we're to seek professional counsel only. Friends may mean well, but

often jump to defend us and may inadvertently encourage a solution that serves more as a retaliation towards the other. Since we're most vulnerable in those moments, we've found it best to consult with people who are trained on ending or preventing relationship combat, not determined to win relationship combat.

4. If any rumors, hearsay, or speculation seems to be valid enough to be taken seriously, it's to immediately become a conversation without postponement or holding anything back. This hasn't been an issue since our college years, but it's good to have an understanding just in case.

5. When we're scared, confused, or unsure about life in general, we pray about it, together. We don't hold it in, we don't vent to anyone in our friend circles or social media; we consult with God. His direction is not only valued but necessary in our lives and since we're now living as one, we also pray as one.

I've found this membrane keeps us away from our natural inclinations to get distracted by the noise outside and keeps life as it naturally progresses from creating a wedge between us. We tweak it as we see necessary from time to time so that it can grow with us, and always serves our mutual goal to serve one another without the interference I've witnessed ruin relationships from the outside in.

Protecting your relationship from the inside out will start with you. First, with self-loving yourself so deeply, consistently, and faithfully that those who want your love can only have what's left over after your cup has already run over, which that will be more than enough. It starts with self and continues through each level of your life, new career, and new person you decide to allow in your circle to enjoy and maximize the happiness you've worked so hard to create. The lessons you learned along the way and the scars you've endured that represent what could not stop you are now a measurement of the royalty you are and standard for which you deserve to be treated. It's because of that, you're not in need of someone to bestow you your crown; you've already earned it, and it's simply your responsibility to never forget it.

The end

Acknowledgments

Years ago, I sat in my small home in Rocky Mount, North Carolina shortly after graduating college. I was officially in the "real world" and I hated it. I had lost the only girl that really meant something to me. I was a 12-hour drive away from my family, and I was working a job selling tobacco, the very thing that took the matriarch of my family away from us. I felt convicted every day I woke up, got dressed for work, and loaded my work laptop into my company vehicle about how I was contributing to more people losing loved ones in their family, and with nothing to come home to that would at least provide some balance, I'd been driven to the coldest floor of rock bottom.

More than ever, I needed the one thing I no longer felt I deserved, which was love. But, in helping complete strangers, I found the next best thing, which was purpose. So, it is to those of you who approached me with an open mind and heart for my messages that I dedicate this book to. Whether you were there on day one, or just heard of me for the first time today, I could never have become who I am, nor who I am still evolving into without you.

There's something about realizing you matter in this world where at times you can feel so small and useless. That something gives new meaning to life, courage to create the version of you that you're proud of, and above all the determination to pass that gift on to others who may have experienced the darkness you once did.

So, thank you for that gift. Thank you for being a part of the catalyst that has changed my life, and as a byproduct, millions of lives across the world. This one is for you. God bless.

P.S. I wrote a chapter that didn't make it in time to be included in the book, but it is just as powerful as the rest of what you've read. I'm going to give it away, absolutely free, to those who do the following two things:

1.) Leave a review on whatever site you purchased this book from. If you bought it in person, then simply type your review in a word document and proceed to the next step.

2.) Email me a screenshot of your review(or the word document) to info@dontforgetyourcrown.com. Give me 12-24 hours to verify your review, and once I do, I will email you the bonus chapter titled, "The Sixth Love Language"

Trust me, if you enjoyed this book, you're going to LOVE this additional chapter. Looking forward to hearing from you, soon. Take care.

CPSIA information can be obtained
at www.ICGtesting.com
Printed in the USA
LVHW031819240619
622207LV00001B/1

9 780991 033676